For my beloved Robert, who has made my entire life possible.

The Boston Globe Illustrated
NEW ENGLAND
GARDENING ALMANAC

A Gardener's Weekly Companion

CAROL STOCKER

The Boston Globe

Above: From the shores of Cape Cod, a beach rose shows its colors. (Boston Globe photo/Jonathan Wiggs)

This book is available in quantity at special discounts for your group or organization. For further information, contact:

Triumph Books
542 S. Dearborn Street
Suite 750
Chicago, Illinois 60605
Phone: (312) 939-3330
Fax: (312) 663-3557

Printed in U.S.A.
ISBN 13: 978-1-57243-871-2
ISBN 10: 1-57243-871-1

EDITOR: Janice Page
ART DIRECTOR/DESIGNER: Wendy Dabcovich
PHOTO RESEARCHERS: Leah Putman, Lisa Tuite

COVER PHOTOS:

FRONT, CLOCKWISE FROM UPPER LEFT: Lilac close-up, Boston Globe photo/ Michele McDonald; tiger swallowtail butterfly on astilbe flower, Boston Globe photo/ John Tlumacki; gourds, Boston Globe photo/ Pam Berry; close-up of a mixed holly wreath, Boston Globe photo/ John Tlumacki.

BACK: It may look alien, but it's just a handful of black pepper. (Boston Globe photo/ Jonathan Wiggs)

Right: A bumblebee visits an herb garden. (Boston Globe photo/ George Rizer)

TABLE OF CONTENTS

Above: Daffodils peek through a picket fence in the heart of Nantucket. (Boston Globe photo/ Mark Wilson)

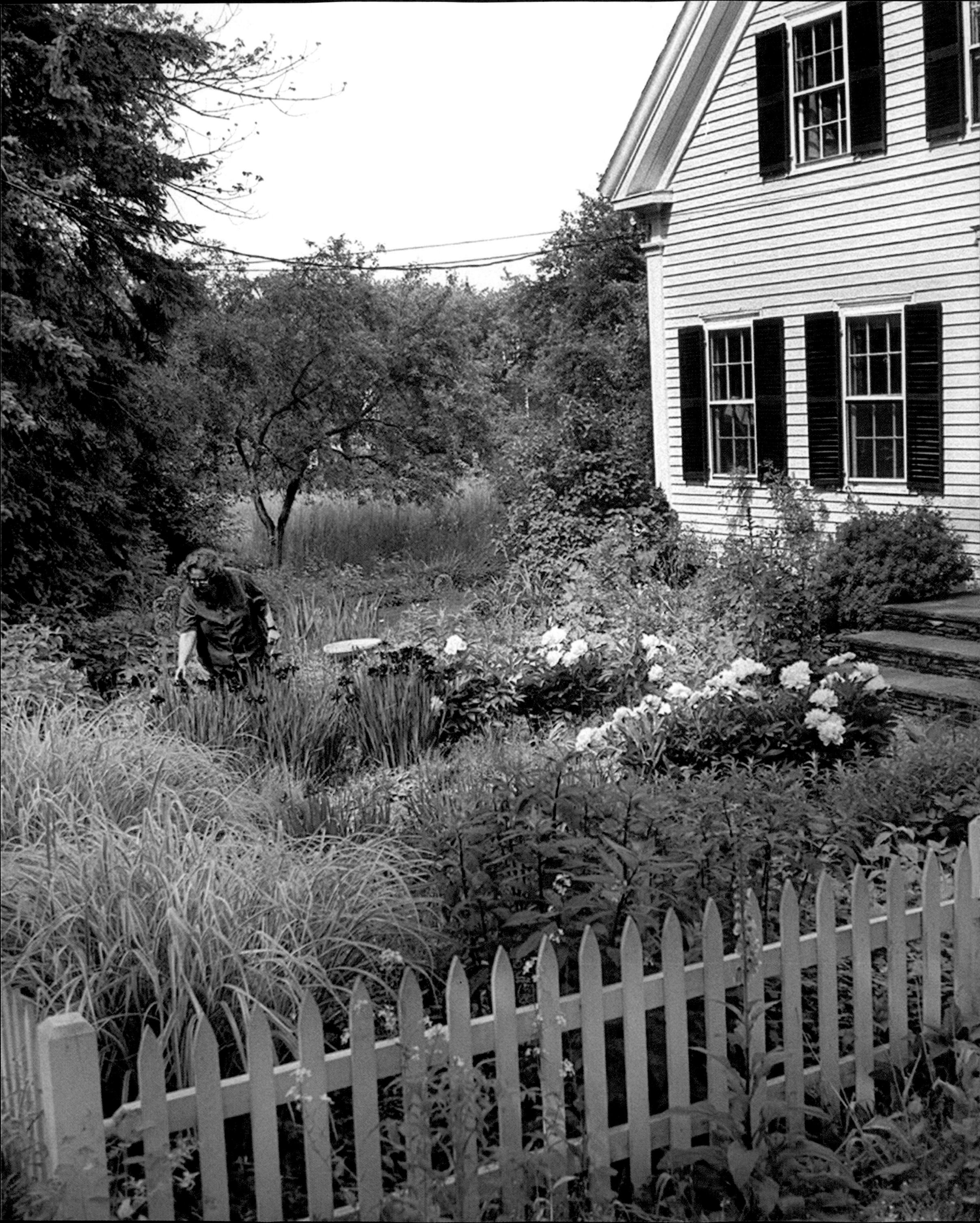

THE GARDEN WRITER'S GARDEN

I EMERGE FROM THE GARDEN DRENCHED IN SWEAT FROM EDGING AND WEEDING in 90-degree weather, I feel wonderful. I'm a powerful warrior princess who has uprooted invaders from my soil and rescued my defenseless flowers. I'm also a little kid who has been playing in the dirt. Never in a million years did I think I would come to enjoy weeding, but I have.

I'm surprised that my enthusiasm has survived almost three decades as a gardener and almost as many years writing about gardening for the Boston Globe. How, with little money, less time and a bad back, have I kept an acre of gardens and orchard from collapsing into tangled disorder?

Left: Author Carol Stocker tends to her perennial garden, where Siberian iris, giant alliums and 70-year-old peonies star in June. (Boston Globe photo/ Pam Berry)

Left to right: Carol Stocker's picket-fenced 'hood is home to Dortmund Kordesii red roses in June and Cimicifuga 'Hillside Black Beauty' in September. (Boston Globe photos/ Pam Berry, Tom Landers)

I admit I actually enjoy teetering on the edge of gardening chaos. I sometimes return from travels to find that some flower beds, especially those farthest from the house, have toppled over that edge. Then I wield once more my weeding weaponry: my asparagus fork, my Cape Cod weeder, my garden claw.

Much of the garden is far back from the house, because our small, antique cottage sits on the road tucked into a corner of the one-acre lot. Originally part of a gentleman's farm in Milton, Massachusetts, the property came with an apple orchard, a butternut-tree allee and an old stone wall. We started colonizing the "out back" with a 100-foot perennial border and a gazebo so far from the house that when we dine al fresco, we think long and hard about hiking back for a salt shaker.

Over the years, we've added two 100-foot mixed shrub and perennial borders; several wildflower gardens; separate hedges of peonies, blueberries and cultivated raspberries; a rose garden; an herb garden; a vegetable plot; a rock garden and a daylily garden; a pergola; and a massive 60-foot-long arbor where we can sit under Concord grapes and clematis. With the help of a landscape designer, we installed a garden of white flowers along the path from the gazebo to help illuminate twilight strolls.

Most of the gardens are hidden from the road by tall grass in the orchard, but in recent years, we've turned our attention toward the view from the road. My husband and I replaced all 1,500 square feet of lawn in our small front yard with a Colonial garden, and I planted the strip of land along the old roadside stone wall. For heavy jobs (remember, bad back), I was lucky to find an invaluable helper with a real feeling for plants. We've been gratified by many compliments from joggers, bicyclists and neighbors, several of whom have created their own front-yard gardens.

My enthusiasm for gardening has stayed constant because the garden itself is constantly changing. It's taken on a life of its own. One night we watch the new moon garden of white flowers come into its own at dusk, twinkling with the lights of the first fireflies. The next night we see two screech owls foraging for their fledgling owlets in our butternut trees. In the morning, I harvest the bouquet du jour: pink roses, spirea and fox gloves, chartreuse lady's mantle, blue catmint and white feverfew.

Though I started out as a frustrated perfectionist, over the years I've learned how to enjoy my garden rather than feel enslaved by it, thanks to a growing know-how and a change in mindset. Though the activity began with painstaking plans made over catalogs on long winter nights, the real-life garden ended up teaching me how to stop thinking. Now I simply respond to the needs of this

and a shade-tolerant garden Solomon's seal (Polygonatum biflorum) that I've never seen in garden centers.

These heirloom plants converted me to old-fashioned cottage garden perennials that seed themselves around so I don't have to plant or divide them, including butterfly weed, European columbine (Aquilegia vulgaris), heliopsis, globe thistle, big foot geraniums (G. macrorrhizum), wild foxgloves (Digitalis purpurea), feverfew (Tanacetum parthenium) and 'Mrs. Moon' lungwort (pulmonaria).

Other perennials that can take a joke if I forget to water include nepeta (the easiest true blue flower), lady's mantle (alchemilla), black-eyed Susan (rudbeckia), artemisias, 'Autumn Joy' sedum, 'Caesar's Brother' Siberian iris and any kind of daylily. Peonies and poppies bloom briefly but are worth it. Giant alliums are the best bulbs.

Instead of hybrid teas, I grow old-fashioned low-maintenance roses such as climber 'Dortmund,' or shrub roses like 'Bonica' and 'Carefree Beauty.'

I can claim success with more demanding plants. 'Pacific Giant' delphiniums teetered and towered for a few years after my husband dug a 2-foot-deep trench of pure compost for these heavy feeders. But once was enough.

When I started gardening, I found it excruciating to wait for something to bloom, and can understand why many people buy shrubs, perennials and even annuals in expensive large sizes. But now I have a huge backlog of plants coming along, so I don't need to pay extra for instant gratification.

Clematis is one example. Most types need to be about eight years old to put on a good show, so people get impatient. But I'm always planting cheap young clematis where they can scramble up lilacs or other shrubs, and each year some forgotten vine I've planted years before treats me to a surprise birthday present. (My birthday's in June!)

I seldom buy more than one of anything. If it works in my garden, it will multiply, or I'll divide it. If it dies, the investment was small. I even divide multi-stemmed shrubs like spireas.

Besides creating a rich environment humming with life, the most rewarding thing about gardening for me is that I can give it away. I love passing along extra plants, sharing the garden with visiting friends, and bringing fresh-cut bouquets to people's homes. The thought delights me that even while I'm at work writing this, there are people passing my garden who enjoy their day a little more because of it. ❀

magic place the way one pets and feeds a mewing cat.

Rather than impose my will on the landscape just because a magazine displayed an exotic hybrid flower that I want to grow, I nurture the soil with compost (instead of fertilizing) and I use only plants that really like it here (instead of ones that look good in pictures). I pull weeds only when they get fat and obvious, but I water and deadhead diligently. Like fashion magazines, the glossier garden publications are breeders of discontent, calling to unrealistic goals. If you want to learn what grows well here in New England, look to your grandparents and neighbors, not to editors in New York.

Of course, I try out many new plants each year. A lot of them die. Years later, I come across their plastic name tags in the soil like little cemetery markers. I never feel guilty. I just chalk it up to "wrong plant, wrong place," and seldom give the same variety a second chance. Weeds have a tremendous will to live, and I demand the same from my garden plants.

Over the long run, much of what's done well are the plants that were growing here originally or that were gifts from other gardeners. My home used to belong to an estate gardener, and I found many heirloom plants, including wild biennial forget-me-not (Myosotis scorpioides), October-blooming monkshood (Aconitum carmichaelii),

MARCH

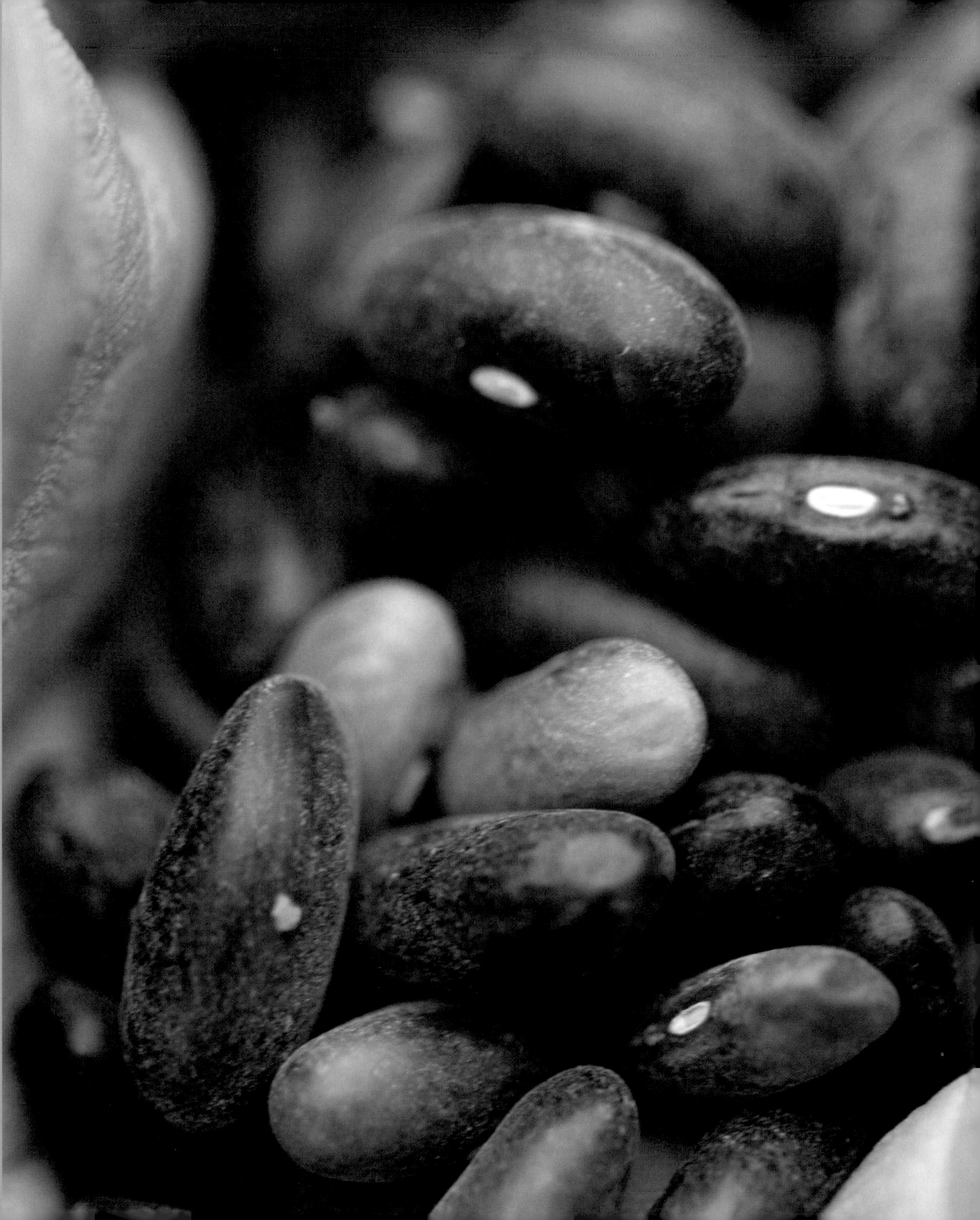

Sowing Seeds of Spring

WHAT COULD BE CHEERIER RIGHT NOW THAN A FEW FLATS OF SEEDLINGS ON THE WINDOWSILL? OK, it's still a bit early, but you can dream and plan and send in those seed orders.

If you're really itching to hurry spring along, you could sow some peppers, kale and lettuce seeds indoors. There are even some seeds you can scatter outdoors now. Johnny jump-ups, corn poppies and Flanders field poppies need a period of cold and will sprout when conditions are right.

Next month, you can start planting seeds of foxgloves, larkspur, radish, spinach, peas and sweet peas outdoors with some hope, if no guarantee, of success. Gardeners love to tempt fate by pushing the climatic envelope. Planting some cool-weather seeds outside is a low-risk enterprise. If they sprout, you plant more. If they die, you plant more.

It's a bigger problem if you start seeds indoors too early. Then you end up with a lot of big plants with no place to go.

Left: A handful of seeds hold the promise of spring. (Boston Globe photo/ Joanne Rathe)

"The most important thing is figuring out when is the right time to plant," says Daniel Cousins, head grower for Nunan the Florist and Greenhouses in Georgetown, MA. "If you stress the plant by having it in too small a container too early, you don't get any advantage. You want the plant to hit the ground at its peak."

So order those seed packs and check the instructions on them to find the right planting time. You should start most vegetables and annual flowers indoors about six weeks before the last spring frost. Memorial Day weekend is considered a safe planting-out date through most of New England and gives you a holiday for planting. In coastal areas, count back from mid-May. Since gardens have their own micro-climates influenced by many factors, it is helpful to keep an annual record of when the last spring frost (and first fall frost) arrives each year where you live.

The most popular vegetable seeds for starting indoors are tomatoes, followed by peppers. Others worth the trouble include broccoli, cabbage, kale, cucumbers, eggplants and lettuce. Don't start root crops such as carrots, beets and turnips indoors. Radishes come up so fast that they don't need the head start anyway. On the other hand, in most of New England the growing season is too short for watermelons, winter squash and pumpkins unless you do sow them indoors (or buy young plants in June).

All this said, don't go overboard with the seed orders. A few flats of seedlings are a lot of fun. More than that is a lot of work.

WHAT YOU NEED

Get some pots, a drip tray for catching water, some kind of label so you don't forget what you've just planted, a clear plastic cover to hold in humidity and a soil-less mix for starting seeds. Digging up soil from your garden only introduces diseases and drainage problems.

Plenty of seed-starting kits are available, and they're great for beginners.

SOWING

If you're using compressed peat pellets such as Jiffy pots, soak them in water until they expand, insert a couple of seeds in each one and stand them in a drip tray.

If you're using a soil-less seed starting mix, fill the seed-starting containers and then water thoroughly. Alternately, you can put water in the potting mix bag and knead it until it has the dampness of a wrung-out sponge, then pour it into your planting containers. Then sow your seeds as directed on the package, the rule of thumb being to sow as deep as the seed is thick.

Some very fine seeds require light to germinate, including columbine, coleus, California poppy, ageratum, sweet alyssum, strawflower, Shasta daisy, sweet rocket and snapdragon. Sow those directly on the surface and cover with about an eighth of an inch of Number 1 filter

Fill containers with a soil-less growing medium.
(Boston Globe photo/ Joanne Rathe)

Cover most seeds with soil as deep as the seed is thick.
(Boston Globe photo/ Joanne Rathe)

sand, which is a coarse but translucent sand that lets light through. The sand holds the seeds in place and helps prevent "damping off," a common fungal disease that can cause seedlings to collapse tragically and can occur when damp soil surface is exposed to spores in the air. A very thin top dressing of parakeet gravel from the supermarket will also protect seedlings from damping off. Make it flush with the rim, using a ruler to scrape off excess.

Label your seed flats as soon as they're planted, as most seedlings look pretty much alike.

Transplant seedlings after they grow two sets of true leaves. (Boston Globe photo/ Joanne Rathe)

WATER, HEAT, HUMIDITY

The soil mix needs to remain constantly moist but not soggy. Cousins avoids sticking his finger in the top of any of the cells to test for moisture. "That's a great way to spread disease," he notes. "Also, the top can be a little dry while the bottom is soaking wet."

Instead, he calculates when to water by weight. "After you've planted and watered your seeds, lift the tray so you know what it feels like damp. All that weight is the moisture. Then, whenever you lift it and the tray feels light, you know you need to water." Since you don't want to disturb the surface, put water in the drip tray.

Most seed-starting kits include a plastic dome to help preserve moisture and humidity. If you don't have one, make your own using a dry-cleaning bag, which is less clingy than plastic wrap, with a straw or chopstick as a tent pole to promote air circulation. Create a few small air holes, too. Beads of moisture on the plastic mean the soil is damp enough.

Most seeds like temperatures in the 70- to 75-degree range to germinate. Artificial light bulbs hung low over them can supply it. Be careful about putting seed flats in a sunny window, though, or they could fry. Seeds actually prefer bottom heat, so use heating mats or just put the flats on top of the refrigerator, which also generates heat. When half the seeds have sprouted, move them to a light source. Sprouts need less warmth, so remove any heating mats after germination.

HELPING THEM GROW

At this point, seedlings need a very sunny window. If you're growing a lot of seeds, you'll need to set up artificial lights. Seedlings need full-spectrum grow lights, not just a couple of 4-foot-long, two-bulb fluorescent shop fixtures from the hardware store. They must be rigged so they're no higher than 6 inches above the seedlings.

If you're a serious seed grower, consider investing in a light stand with stacked shelves of height adjustable tube lights that provide light to the seedlings below them and bottom heat to the germinating seeds above them.

Keep the growing medium moist and thin the seedlings as needed by snipping off unwanted sprouts at the soil line with manicure scissors. (Don't pull them out; you risk disturbing the roots of the remaining seedling.) You should be left with one good seedling per compartment.

After seeds have developed a set of true leaves, give them half-strength liquid fertilizers every two weeks.

TRANSPLANTING

If you sowed your seeds in one large container of soil-less mix, you'll need to transplant them to individual pots after they grow two sets of true leaves. (Don't count the first embryonic leaves they sprouted, called "cotyledons" or "seed leaves.") You may also need to transplant seedlings to a larger pot if they outgrow their original container (because you started them too early?). Always handle seedlings by their leaves, not their stems. If you tear a leaf, the plant will grow another; if you damage the stem, it's done for.

MOVING ON OUT

A week before your seedlings are due to be planted, move them for about an hour to a spot outdoors that's sheltered from wind. Repeat this all week, leaving them outdoors for an hour longer each day.

If you have a cold frame, all you have to do is move your seedlings into it, and open the lid when the temperatures in the cold frame rise above 65, and close it when they fall. Some cold frames do this automatically.

Once your seedlings are planted in the garden, the promise of spring will have become a reality. ✱

IF YOU SPENT ANY TIME IN COASTAL MASSACHU-SETTS IN 1981, you probably remember an invasion of gypsy moth caterpillars so dramatic that it literally stopped trains and caused car accidents. Well don't relax your guard, because the slimy assault continues. Only these days, gypsy moths have given way to hordes of Eastern tent caterpillars, fall cankerworms and forest tent caterpillars.

The main culprit now is a European insect new to the East Coast. It's called the winter moth because the adult moths emerge from their cocoons in late November and December. If you had a snowstorm of these tiny moths at your porch lights last Christmas, your trees are in for trouble, thanks to their voracious offspring.

Labeled Operophtera brumata, the winter moth multiplies because it has no natural enemies in New England. Even though females are flightless, the insect has managed to spread to where individual banded maples and oaks have yielded up to 1,600 females laying eggs on each

tree monitored. Since winter moths can lay 150 eggs, that adds up to almost a quarter of a million caterpillars per tree. Many of these inchworms may starve to death, especially if they hatch before the tree buds swell, "but it's going to get worse for the next five years, at least," says Joseph Elkinton, forest entomologist and ecologist at UMass-Amherst.

By then, if all goes according to plan, a counter measure will start kicking in. Elkinton is raising a predator of the winter moth called Cyzenis albicans, a fly released in Nova Scotia to control a winter moth outbreak there 50 years ago. But the moths have a big head start. "It took five years for them to multiply enough to catch up with the winter moth population when they were released in Nova Scotia," Elkinton says.

Until then, you're on your own, and trees that have been defoliated for several years are very unhappy. They face decline and even death without extra help.

The tiny green inchworms start with oaks, maples, fruit trees, ash, rose of Sharon and blueberry bushes, but almost

Above: The male winter moth, drawn to outdoor lights on November and December evenings. Left: A quarter million inchworms can hatch on a single tree. (Photos courtesy of Robert D. Childs, UMass Amherst)

Take the following steps to help your trees survive. They also work on other caterpillars, but most will hatch a bit later than winter moths and have a longer feeding period when they can be sprayed.

• **Contact a licensed arborist about spraying large trees before they get too busy to reach. To find state-certified arborists, visit certifiedtreeandlawn.org.**

• **Consider using an eco-friendly horticultural dormant oil. Sprayed before winter moths hatch around April 20, it will smother many of the eggs. Use only when temperatures exceed 45 degrees and the forecast is for 48 hours above freezing so the oil has time to dry. Apply sprays containing Spinosad during the caterpillars' vulnerable period, after leaf buds open in early May, exposing the caterpillars inside, but before they stop eating in late May.**

• **Water defoliated trees over the entire root zone weekly through July and August. (Set out a tuna fish can for measuring an inch of water.) Watering is very important.**

• **Have your trees sprayed twice by a state certified arborist with two applications of Spinosad, which is found in Conserve, Bulls-Eye BioInsecticide, or Monterey Garden Spray, once right after the tree leaves begin to open in early May and a second time one to two weeks later.**

Left to right: Female winter moths have unusable stunted wings; caterpillars can leave maple tree foliage in tatters. (Photos courtesy of Robert D. Childs, UMass Amherst)

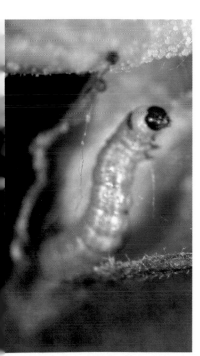

The males just flutter around and mate with the flightless females, who clamber up trees, lay eggs, and die.

Left: Leaves open in May to reveal inchworms that weaseled their way inside leaf buds to feed. (Photo courtesy of Robert D. Childs, UMass Amherst)

any leaves or flowers are fair game after that. One way to tell if you're going to be hit hard is to check tree trunks for the tiny orange eggs the moths randomly scatter in bark crevices. Just before they hatch, the eggs turn bright red.

The winter moth inchworms can hatch anytime between mid March and late April, depending upon the season's accumulated warmth. They immediately weasel their way inside swelling leaf buds, where they cannot be reached by sprays. The leaves open in tatters. After that, the caterpillars are "free feeders"; they spread by swinging tree to tree like Tarzans on their own silken ropes.

Winter moth caterpillars are active for only about three or four weeks. Between mid May and mid June, again depending on temperatures, they will dangle down to the ground on skeins of silk and burrow into the top layer of soil, where they will become dormant pupae until emerging as adult moths between Thanksgiving and New Year's for their nighttime mating ritual. They don't eat anything then. The males just flutter around and mate with the flightless females, who clamber up trees, lay eggs, and die. Then next April those eggs will hatch ... and on and on it goes. ✿

Above: Pussy willow catkins open gray, then turn yellow with pollen. (Boston Globe photo/ Michele McDonald)

Left: Small species crocuses open 10 days earlier than the larger Dutch crocus. (Photo courtesy of Netherlands Bulb Information Center)

Right: A mighty mite 4-inch tall crocus surveys Boston's Trinity Church and John Hancock Tower. (Boston Globe photo/ John Tlumacki)

GARDENER'S WEEK 1

Early flowers: Look for the earliest spring flowers. Spidery yellow witch hazel blooms will lead the parade, followed by the nodding bells of snowdrops and hellebores, fuzzy pussy willows, yellow Cornelian dogwood and spicebush, colorful crocus, white forsythia (abeliophyllum) and the white bells of Japanese pieris.

Fruit: When weather permits, prune apple trees and blueberry shrubs to allow light into their interior branches. Cut out raspberry canes that fruited last year. Prune grapes before the buds open or the sap will bleed. Remove about three-quarters of the canes from established vines. Leave the older wood, which is dark with peeling bark, but prune off all but four of the new canes, which are pencil thin, smooth and lighter colored. Then cut those remaining canes back part way, too. Don't forget to remove any Christmas lights first. They've been up too long already.

Onions: Sow leek and onion seeds indoors now or they won't get big enough by harvest time. If they get too tall to fit under grow lights before transplanting outdoors, give them a "haircut" with scissors.

Ornamental ponds: Don't feed fish when the ice first melts; they're still dormant and uneaten food will contaminate the pond. Don't resume feeding until the water temperature rises to 50 degrees.

Seeds: Read garden catalogs, send in seed orders and assemble your seed-starting setup and paraphernalia. If you're just learning to start seeds indoors, order easy-to-grow varieties such as basil, coreopsis, annual phlox, cosmos, dianthus, gaillardia, gloriosa daisy, marigold, yarrow and zinnias.

Snow thrower: Add a fuel stabilizer to what you think may be the season's last tank of fuel, then run the engine for at least five minutes to circulate the conditioned fuel.

Vegetables: Use restraint when planning a vegetable garden. You can never have too many flowers, but you can definitely plant too many zucchinis. So consider how much your family can eat, unless you will can or freeze the extras. Just two plants each of summer squash, winter squash, eggplant and long-yielding indeterminate tomatoes are enough to feed one person. Figure on no more than 12 lettuce plants, 15 bean plants, 20 beets, 30 carrots, four cucumber vines, five pea plants, 12 spinach plants and 10 radishes per person over the course of a year. Stagger planting times so that all the plants of one type of vegetable don't mature at once, especially lettuce.

TOP 10

Obstacles to gardening in New England:

10 **Rainy spring weekends. They never had them in Camelot.**

9 **Rocks. Almost 400 years of digging, and we still haven't got them all out.**

8 **Acid rain. Air mailed from the nation's Rust Belt.**

7 **No see'ums. Stealth attack.**

6 **Mosquitoes. At least you can see those.**

5 **Skin cancer. The good news is that gardeners have a lower rate of osteoporosis due to sun exposure.**

4 **Poison ivy. Very irritating.**

3 **Late frosts. Nipped in the bud.**

2 **Early frosts. Harvesting by flashlight.**

1 **Mud. The fifth New England season.**

GARDENER'S WEEK 2

Annuals: Seeds you can actually start indoors now include verbena, snapdragons, salvia and ageratum. You can also sow most perennial seeds indoors because these frost-hardy plants can be planted outside in late April. But hold back from planting warmth-loving annuals, or they'll be too spindly from lack of daylight before it's warm enough to set them outside.

Cleanup: Cut ornamental grasses to the ground and compost the tops. New shoots will soon sprout.

Houseplants: This is a good time to repot plants before they hit their spring growth spurt.

Lawns: Beat the spring rush and take your lawn mower to a repair shop for blade sharpening and a tune-up. Have them replace worn belts, spark plugs and air filters, and change the transmission fluid, oil, oil filter and engine coolant.

Pruning: This is a useful outdoor activity if you're itching to work outdoors now. Trim off any broken branches so the ragged ends don't encourage disease. Cut back red-twigged dogwood almost all the way to old wood so it will produce more colorful young stems. Prune rose of Sharon back a third. Lightly pruning bayberry, cotoneaster, firethorn, fruiting viburnums and other fall ornamentals will increase the production of colorful berries this fall. Now through April is also a good time to lightly prune magnolias, mountain ashes, redbuds, shadblow, fringe trees, hawthorns, crab apples and golden rain trees. Bring some of the cuttings indoors, recut the stems and soak them overnight in a warm bath and then put them in a vase of slightly hot water to see if you can get some blooms or foliage to open early. Do not prune spring-flowering shrubs such as April-blooming bridal wreath spireas, quinces, forsythias, mock oranges, honeysuckles, flowering cherries, lilacs, pieris, azaleas or rhododendrons unless you want a few stems to try to force in a vase for early bloom indoors. Otherwise wait until after they've bloomed this spring or you'll sacrifice some of this year's flowers. Also, don't prune maples, beeches and birches except for a bit of flower arranging material, as they tend to bleed when cut.

Vegetables: Start seeds of lettuce, Swiss chard, kale, collards and cabbage indoors under grow lights or on a south facing windowsill, and constantly keep them slightly moist until they sprout. A very fine top layer of parakeet gravel or Number 2 chicken grit from a feed store will help prevent "damping off" fungus, as will a fan to gently circulate the air. Breeze-rustled seedlings also develop sturdier roots.

Above photos, left to right:

Siberian squill

Snowdrops

Snow crocuses

More Siberian squill

Eranthis

Eranthis and snowdrops

(Photos courtesy of Netherlands Bulb Information Center)

GARDENER'S WEEK 3

Hellebores: These perennials have gotten a lot of hype, but don't worry if yours aren't blooming yet. These are long-lived plants and, like peonies, they take several years in the ground before they perform well. They'll look better if you snip off last year's battered foliage carefully without hurting emerging shoots.

Hemlocks: Look for tiny white balls along the stems on the undersides of hemlock needles, which signify hemlock wooly adelgid (Adeles tsugae), a new pest fatal to hemlocks. If the cottony egg masses are present, spray the tree thoroughly with horticultural oil on a day when temperatures are above 40 degrees, or call an arborist for treatment.

Lawns: Frost seeding is a clever trick for patching lawns. Sprinkle grass seeds where you need them on mornings when the top of the soil is crystalline and crunchy to walk on. The seeds will sink into the open slivers in the earth and be happily tucked underground when the ice melts and the expanding soil closes up.

Maple sugaring: Tap sugar maple trees on a sunny day with a temperature of at least 40 degrees, immediately after a night when the thermometer fell below 25 degrees. This fluctuation is key. Never tap a sugar maple that's less than 10 inches in diameter.

Mulch: Begin removing burlap wrappings from evergreens and winter mulches such as needled boughs and salt hay.

Tools: It's time to clean out the tool shed and think about what didn't work and what to invest in for the season. Essential tools include a heavy-duty iron bow rake; a long-handled, round-pointed shovel; a square garden spade; a stirrup hoe (or scuffle hoe); hand pruners and a belt-mounted scabbard to hold them; a long-handled lopper for larger branches; a small, curved pruning saw; and a collapsible lawn rake. If you live on a wooded lot, buy a bucksaw that can be used to prune larger branches or brush. If your soil is hardpan or loaded with rocks, get a pickax. Get a mill file about 8 inches long to sharpen spades, trowels and hoes. (Draw the file across the beveled surface of each blade at a 30 degree angle, pushing the file away from you. Oil the blade once it's sharp and wipe it with a clean rag to prevent rust.)

Vegetables: Cold-hardy vegetables you can start now indoors from seed include kale and lettuce. You can also start peas in biodegradable peat pots that can be planted directly outdoors to minimize transplant trauma next month.

Above photos, left to right:

Pushkinia

Crocuses

Pussy willow 'Weeping Sally'

Iris reticulata

Glory of the Snow

(Photos courtesy of Netherlands Bulb Information Center, www.parkseed.com)

GARDENER'S WEEK 4

Annuals: Start seeds of nicotiana (flowering tobacco), portulaca, China aster, dwarf marigold, ageratum, cleome and petunia.

Birds: Put up bird boxes to attract nesters, or set nesting materials (pet or human hair or lint from the dryer, for example) on the ground, in a tree crotch or in a hanging bag with holes.

Bulbs: Discard bulbs you've grown in water, such as hyacinth or paperwhite narcissus, after they finish blooming. Except for tulips, hardy bulbs that grew in pots of soil during the winter can be planted outdoors in April at a depth three times the height of the bulb. Don't remove the leaves. Throw out any bulbs you bought last fall and failed to plant.

Cleanup: Pick up sticks and other yard debris.

Forcing flowering shrubs: Sick of winter? Cut branches of flowering quince, amelanchier, magnolia, lilac, red maple, redbud, PJM rhododendron, cherry, fothergilla, pear or forsythia on a day when the temperature is above freezing. For interesting catkins, cut willows, birches, beeches and filberts. Remove leaves and buds from the lower 6 inches and recut the stems under warm water at a severe angle, an inch above the original cut. For branches wider than a half inch, make a 1-inch slit 2 inches up the length of the stems. If possible, soak the entire boughs overnight in a warm bath before placing the stems in a bucket of hot water that's comfortable to the touch. Set them where temperatures are cool, ideally 45 to 55 degrees, then change the water weekly.

Hydrangeas: If you protected the buds of blue hydrangeas from desiccation by winter winds by covering the entire plant with a mound of bark mulch, carefully remove the mulch now and spread it in a 4-inch-deep layer around the plant, making sure the mulch does not come in contact with any stems.

Mulch: Continue pulling back winter mulch from on top of sprouting bulbs and perennials in two stages, a week apart, so foliage is not scorched by unaccustomed light. Newly exposed young yellow leaves will green up quickly.

Soil improvement: Spread a 2- to 4-inch layer of compost over the garden at least two weeks before you intend to start planting. If you don't have a compost pile, order finished compost for delivery from a garden center, telling them how many square feet of garden space you have. If you don't need enough to meet a minimum bulk order, purchase bags of compost or dehydrated manure.

Vegetables: Start seeds of peppers and eggplants indoors using bottom heat from a heat pad to increase their germination and growth rate. Soak okra seeds for 24 hours in warm water before planting this week or next. Start seeds of broccoli and cauliflower indoors.

KNOW YOUR TERMS

ANNUAL: A short-lived plant that completes its lifecycle of sprouting, growing, blooming, setting seed and dying in a single year.

BIENNIAL: A plant with a two-year lifecycle that sprouts the first year but blooms, sets seed and dies the following year.

PERENNIAL: A long-lived plant that dies to the ground each winter but usually sprouts new growth for two or more springs.

TENDER PERENNIAL: A normally long-lived plant that can't survive winters outdoors where you live.

TROPICAL: A plant from warm regions that can't survive heavy frost.

Lenten rose
(Helleborus hybridus).

This long-blooming member of the buttercup family has very early 2-inch cuplike flowers in many fascinating color combinations of mauve, white and green. It thrives without attention in partial shade. A long-lived plant, it takes several years to reach full size.

(Photo courtesy of www.parkseed.com)

APRIL

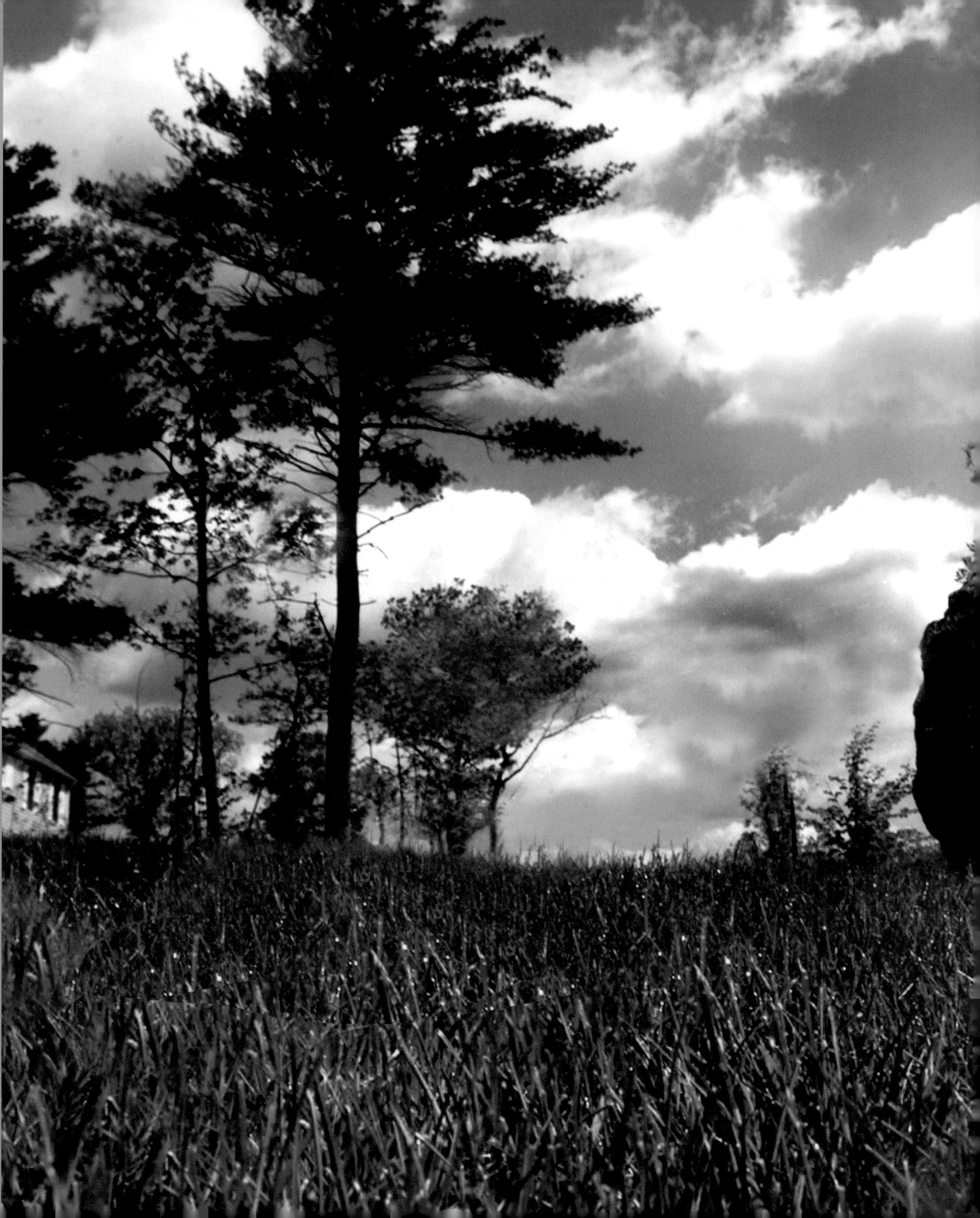

THE DO-IT-YOURSELF LAWN

MANY PEOPLE'S MOST IMPORTANT LAWN CARE QUESTION IS WHOM SHOULD THEY HIRE TO TAKE CARE OF IT. Unfortunately, the lawn industry has been slow to respond to public unease about the overuse of toxic lawn chemicals. Though more lawn care companies are paying lip service to such concerns, it can be difficult to find ones that really invest the time and skill required to be environmentally friendly.

If you can pay someone to mow, fine. My advice is to do the rest of the lawn care yourself. No one cares about your lawn more than you. Why pay to keep lawn technicians working March to December when your family and the environment are not exactly benefiting from the unnecessary chemicals your land must absorb to keep them so busy?

Left: The grass awakens from winter dormancy and reaches for the sky. (Boston Globe photo/ Barry Chin)

Surprisingly little needs to be done if you can tolerate a lawn that is less than putting-green perfect. The only two things on the "must do" list are raking leaves and mowing. The other operations are apt to create more problems than they solve.

So here's a brief primer on common-sense, low-chemical lawn care:

FERTILIZER

Lawn grass is perennial, while most lawn weeds are annuals. Lawn companies like to apply fertilizer in the spring because it helps the lawn to green up more quickly, but this means you're also feeding the weeds. That's why I recommend fertilizing only in September or October, when most weeds are dying off and the grass roots will get all those nutrients. As with most gardening, your goal should be to encourage root rather than top growth.

When you do fertilize, use a slow-acting natural-based fertilizer that improves the soil over time. Organic fertilizers also have more trace elements and won't burn your lawn.

Avoid quick-acting chemical fertilizers, which tend to acidify the soil. This hurts earthworms and soil micro-organisms that aerate your lawn and prevent thatch buildup. If you kill them off with too many chemicals, you'll just have to pay someone else to do their job.

Too much fertilizer, especially lots of nitrogen, also makes grass more vulnerable to drought, pests and disease by making it grow faster than it wants to naturally. Also, when lawns get more nitrogen than they can use, the extra gets washed into local waterways, where it stimulates runaway algae growth that suffocates fish. A green lawn may be beautiful, but a scummy pond isn't.

If your lawn is already dependent on chemical fertilizers, wean it off gradually by using a small amount of low-nitrogen fertilizer during your transitional year.

If you see a dog peeing on your lawn, water that spot immediately.

Speaking of fertilizer, let's not forget dog urine, which is great in small amounts. Usually, however, it's delivered in one concentrated spot and kills the grass. If you see a dog peeing on your lawn, water that spot immediately. Dilution is the solution. This works even several hours after the dastardly event, so if you have a particular area that is favored by neighborhood canines (or your own), try to water it daily.

SOIL AMENDMENTS

Your lawn is more apt to need an application of lime than fertilizer. Grass can't make full use of nutrients unless the soil has a pH between 6.5 and 6.7. Calcium is also one of the secrets of a low-maintenance lawn, so try to find calcitic lime rather than the more common dolomitic lime. Applying a thin layer of horticultural gypsum also will raise your soil's calcium level. Use a cyclone spreader for separate

Above: Acid rain has increased the need to lime lawns, but test your soil's pH first. Lawns like a slightly alkaline pH of 6.5 to 6.7. (Boston Globe photo/ Wendy Maeda)

applications of pelletized lime and gypsum if a standard spreader leaves you with "lawn stripes." Don't buy topsoil unless you have an excellent source, because it's usually full of weed seeds.

SOIL TESTING

To find out how much lime to apply and what, if any, fertilizer is needed, buy a kit to test your soil. You can also send samples to your state soil-testing lab, or some garden centers will do tests for you.

WEED CONTROL

Herbicides that kill weed seeds before they sprout are much less toxic than poisons applied after weeds have sprouted. Apply a pre-emergent crabgrass control when the yellow forsythia is in bloom. Don't use a pre-emergent herbicide if you're planting grass seed, though, or that will be killed, too.

Set your mower high and you'll have fewer weeds. The

fashion for close-cropped lawns weakens the grass and gives weeds the edge. Letting your grass stay at 2 1/2 to 3 inches allows it to out-compete weeds, and the lawn still will be springy under foot.

SEEDING

If your lawn is patchy, don't replace it; thicken it. Rent a seed slicer that will plant your grass seed at the appropriate depth. Fill the hopper with seed and run it over your lawn a couple of times, approaching from different angles. Alternatively, use a spreader and rake it in. If you're patching a bare spot, cover the seeded area with a 1/4 inch of compost.

Choose a grass seed mix that suits your needs. For instance, consider a "sports turf" mix for areas with heavy foot traffic.

Look for new cultivars of perennial ryegrass and fescues that contain endophytes to increase their tolerance of drought and surface-feeding insects such as chinch bugs. The best all-purpose, cool-season grasses for New England are the fine fescues.

Most new grasses are so vigorous that they'll crowd out your old lawn, so don't worry about matching the new seed to the existing grass if you over-seed.

Once planted, grass seeds must be kept constantly moist until each has sprouted a couple of leaves, or they'll die. This takes about a month. Spring rains help, but when they're absent you'll need to water daily. After the first couple of weeks, you can apply a starter fertilizer formulated for lawn seedlings. Don't mow until the new grass reaches 3 inches.

MOWING

This is the most important thing you do for your lawn. Do it high and often, once a week until July, when growth rates slow. If you trim less than an inch off the top, leave the fresh clippings on the lawn, where they quickly disappear and serve as organic fertilizer.

Because they don't have catalytic converters, gas-powered mowers produce as much air pollution in an hour as a car driven 350 miles. If you're concerned about the environment, you like exercise, and your lawn isn't too large, consider one of the old-fashioned reel mowers that have come back into fashion. If you're not up to all that pushing, there are new electric mowers, which are almost equally quiet and non-polluting. ❁

Right: Gardener Tom McCafferty knows the drill: Mow high, mow frequently, and leave clippings on the lawn. (Boston Globe photo/ Pat Greenhouse)

HE MOWS THEM DOWN AT FENWAY

TO MANY LAWN LOVERS, A MAJOR LEAGUE BASEBALL FIELD ON A SPRING DAY is the most brilliant example of turf science in all of sports. And David Mellor, the director of grounds for the Boston Red Sox, has upped the ante with his complex mowing patterns.

To the game's arsenal of grassy stripes and checkerboards, he's added stars, wavy lines, wedges, diamonds, bull's-eyes and numbers, all created with rollers attached to the mower that bend strips of grass in opposite directions to create contrasting light refractions. For his Opening Day debut at Fenway in 2001, Mellor mowed a pattern of large and small diamonds.

He hails from Ohio, where his widowed mother raised him as a Red Sox fan in the long tradition of his father's family. A car accident more than two decades ago mangled Mellor's right knee and ended his youthful dream of coming to Boston as a player, but he found another way.

As assistant director of grounds for the Milwaukee Brewers, Mellor helped design the playing field for Miller Park stadium. But he was only there three days when the Sox called him up.

"It's the dream of my life," he says, pointing to two empty seats near the dugout. "Those were my dad's regular seats when he used to take my brother to games here."

Now Mellor manages the unique micro-climate of Fenway Park, where the warmest, sunniest spot is not the stands or the playing field, but the left-field wall known as the Green Monster (which is why it's a great spot to pile snow to melt).

His trademark mowing patterns are the result of serendipity, ingenuity, and former Beatle Paul McCartney, whose rainy 1993 concert at the old Milwaukee County Stadium left the outfield with an unsightly dark strip. Mellor mowed eye-catching, intricate patterns in the

Left and far left: David Mellor always dreamed of joining the Red Sox. Now his creative mowing patterns spread from ball fields to backyards. (Boston Globe photos/ George Rizer, Dominic Chavez)

Below: Saucer magnolias signal Opening Day in Boston. (Boston Globe photo/ Tom Landers)

infield to draw attention away from the damage, igniting a friendly competition among clubs to mow the most original designs. "I didn't invent it," Mellor says. "But I took it to the next level."

Mellor has become so adept at freestyle mowing that he created one famous pattern of wavy lines (designed by his daughter when she was 6 years old) in only 40 minutes. "The trick," he says, "is to focus on a distant object and drive toward it." Otherwise, he uses chalk, string or computer to chart complex designs before mowing.

Patterned mowing is catching on beyond ballparks, too. Mellor often hears from groundskeepers and homeowners who want the secrets of his techniques. His creative patterns were pictured in a traveling show about lawn art, and he's done a book called "Picture Perfect: Mowing Techniques for Lawns, Landscapes, and Sports," (Sleeping Bear Press, 2001).

But face it, Mellor has many advantages over the average home gardener. Underground pipes drain water from the Fenway turf, and the infield has warmed up and greened up under a permeable thermal blanket that serves the purpose of a greenhouse. How else could Fenway's grass be ready for play when you can barely walk on your lawn without leaving squishy footprints? ❁

GARDENER'S WEEK 1

Begonias: Start tuberous begonias indoors in a light potting soil away from strong light.

Brassicas: Lime soils where members of the brassica family such as cauliflower, cabbage and broccoli will be planted to help avoid problems with club root. Once this disease, which misshapes roots, appears in the soil, it can remain there for years, so change (rotate) where you plant these crops each year.

Bulbs: Scatter bulb fertilizer around sprouted bulb foliage.

Cleanup: Cut back the dead tops of perennials left over from last year. Finish pulling back winter mulch from perennials so it's not in direct contact with the stems. Be careful not to damage emerging leaves. Rake winter debris from lawns and flower beds when the soil is not damp. A bamboo or other springy kind of rake is less apt to tear sod.

Insect pests: Spray fruit trees, hollies, junipers and arborvitae with dormant oil (which is organic and nontoxic) to smother the eggs of insect pests. If winter moths swarmed your porch lights last winter, spray the branches and trunks of leafless trees, especially fruit trees and maples, for partial control of their offspring. Spray on a day when temperatures stay above 40 degrees for several hours to allow the dormant oil to dry rather than freeze.

Iris borers: The insects hatch after two consecutive 70-degree days, making that the optimum time to spray bearded iris with a mild Permethrin-based insecticide such as Bonide's Borer-Miner Killer or organic Bulls-Eye BioInsecticide. Bearded (aka German) iris have sword-like leaves and furry "beards" in the center of their multicolored lower petals, and are the most colorful, popular and pest prone of the several kinds of garden iris. If you want something more low maintenance, plant Siberian iris.

Organic lawn care: New England lawns only need fertilization in the fall, so don't apply nitrogen for quick greening. It often ends up in local waterways, where it suffocates aquatic life by stimulating algae grown.

Pansies: These can be purchased and planted outside now. Pinch off each flower as the spent petals curl and the round green ovary at the base of the flower starts to swell and they will continue to bloom until it gets hot, and even longer if you buy heat-resistant varieties. Medium-blue-colored pansies work best with other flowers in the garden.

Parsnips: If you have some left in the ground from last year, dig them up now for harvesting before they resume growth and lose flavor.

Roses: Pull back soil around bulging grafts if you hilled up around the trunk to protect the plant last fall. Plant new roses this month so they'll bloom this year. Fertilize.

Vegetables: Fertilize seedlings with half-strength water-soluble fertilizer twice a week after the first true leaves emerge. These have an appearance more characteristic of the plant species than the very first leaves to open, which are temporary (cotyledons). Thin crowded seedlings by snipping off the weakest stems with scissors. Sow spinach, lettuce and radish outdoors.

Annual flowers: Plant seeds of larkspur, bachelor's buttons, Shirley poppies, and sweet peas outdoors.

Above photos, left to right:

Magnolias in Boston's Back Bay, where each April the mature trees present a festival of blooms.

(Boston Globe photos/ Pam Berry, Yunghi Kim)

GARDENER'S WEEK 2

Fruit trees: Fertilize pear and apple trees.

Irrigation systems: Flush out your sprinkler or drip system when you first turn it on. During the winter, many critters take up residence in emitters, tubes and pipes and get stuck. Open the ends of drip tubes and flush by turning on the water. For sprinklers, remove the nozzles from the last head on each pipe and run the water for at least an hour. When done, make sure standing water doesn't drain back into the pipes, taking the dirt back with it.

Lawn: This is the time to over-seed or re-seed your lawn. Apply a pre-emergent crabgrass control when the yellow forsythia is in bloom. Don't use it if you're planting grass seed, however.

Peas: Sow peas or transplant pea seedlings outside. Plant taller pea varieties 1 to 2 inches apart along an A-frame trellis or next to a wire fence you use to enclose your garden. As you sow the seed, sprinkle an inoculant in the row to help increase the plant's growth and nitrogen fixing ability. (Don't do this in advance.) Then cover and water well. You won't need to thin the seedlings. If the plants are growing on a trellis, guide the young stems at first by tying. For a longer harvest, sow a succession of seeds every one or two weeks until mid-May, or combine early with midseason and late varieties planted all at once. Don't plant edible pea and ornamental sweet pea seeds together as sweet pea seeds are toxic and it's difficult to tell them apart. Harvest the pods of snap peas and snow peas when they're small, to eat whole.

Perennials: If you're applying a granular chemical fertilizer, sprinkle it around emerging plants, not on top of them.

Roses: When new leaf buds become visible, spray roses with dormant oil when weather is above 40 degrees to create a protective barrier. Prune out dead wood and crossed stems.

Soil preparation: Don't work soil until you can squeeze it in your fist and have it break apart easily rather than remain in a mud ball. Otherwise, you risk compacting the soil rather than loosening it. When it's dry enough, remove weeds and spade in some compost and peat moss, which will both enrich and loosen the soil.

Trees and shrubs: These can be purchased and planted now. Apply organic Bacillus thuringiensis (B.t.) if you see inch worms. It works best on young ones.

Vegetables: Start seeds of tomato and basil indoors under lights. Keep the growing mixture very slightly damp to the touch. You can sow seeds of spinach, peas, radishes, turnips, chives, beets and lettuce outdoors if the soil is warm and dry enough. Soak parsnip seeds for a day before sowing outdoors a half inch deep. Germination rate is poor, so sow heavily. Because parsnip seeds are slow to sprout, many people mix them with fast-growing radish seeds to mark the spot and provide a double harvest. Seeds may rot if the soil is below 40 degrees, so use a soil thermometer to judge when to plant, or plant subsequent weekly sowings to be safe. Cover seedlings on frosty nights with a lightweight sheet or with floating row covers of lightweight spun polyester.

GARDENER'S WEEK 3

Annuals: Some go on sale too early. Ask which varieties have been "hardened off," meaning they've gradually acclimated to colder outside temperatures. Start seeds of zinnias, celosia and cosmos indoors.

Bulbs: Sprinkle a bulb fertilizer around emerging bulb foliage. Deadhead (which means cut, pinch or snap off spent blossoms) your daffodils, hyacinths and tulips when they finish blooming, but let leaves and stems remain. Don't bother deadheading minor (small) bulbs such as pushkinia and squill; they often self-seed. Spray tulips frequently with a repellant if you have deer. Dig up and divide crowded snowdrops now.

Dahlias: If you saved last year's tubers, you can get a head start on this year's flowers by planting them indoors in pots. Tubers can be divided with a sharp knife as long as each remains attached to a piece of stem. Water once and store in a warm, dark place until they sprout, then continue watering and plant outdoors in late May.

Fertilizer: The three numbers on the label indicate the amounts of nitrogen (N) for leaf growth, phosphorus (P), and potassium (K) for flower and root growth as well as disease resistance. Other essential macronutrients that are often missing from chemical fertilizers include calcium, carbon, magnesium and sulphur. Plants also need tiny amounts of boron, chlorine, copper, iron, manganese, molybdenum and zinc. Many of these are found in compost, well-rotted manure, rock phosphate and greensand, so add some when you plant. A little limestone is also a good amendment (except for acid-loving plants such as blueberries and rhododendrons) because it buffers the effects of acid rain.

Forsythia: The best time to prune forsythia is immediately after blooming, because new buds are formed by early June. The branch tips of forsythia will root where they touch the ground if not pruned back, creating a jumbled thicket.

Poison ivy: Always use gloves and protective clothing when working around its stems and roots, which can cause dermatitis even when leafless or dead. Use soap or detergent to wash any clothing or tools that may have had contact with poison ivy. Spray poison ivy with herbicide while the leaves are young and red.

Vegetables: Harden off seedlings of frost-resistant spring vegetables for outdoor planting if you've grown your own. One week before planting, place the trays of seedlings outdoors for a few hours in a shady and wind-protected spot. Increase the sun exposure and time outside each day until planting. Do this now with seedlings of onions, leeks, lettuce, Swiss chard, kale, collards and cabbage. Purchased seedlings of these vegetables should already be hardened off and ready for planting. Direct sow seeds of carrots, dill, beets, parsnips, potatoes, radishes, spinach, collard greens, brassicas, fennel and Swiss chard outdoors. Rotate your crops on a three-year cycle so you don't plant the same kind of vegetable in the same place each year. Placing a floating row cover over these crops will help get them off to a good start. Make a last spring sowing of spinach.

Weeds: These are often among the first plants to emerge, so are easiest to find and weed out now.

GARDENER'S WEEK 4

Brown evergreens: Don't give up on them. Winter wind may have sucked the moisture out of their leaves, but most will produce new leaves this spring. Water them when temperatures are above freezing. Sometimes individual branches die and need to be pruned out. Lightly scrape the bark with your thumbnail. If the wood is still alive you should see traces of green underneath. When in doubt, wait until mid-June before removing seemingly dead branches or plants.

Cleanup: Redefine the boundaries of garden beds and borders with an edging tool.

Dandelions: They're starting to bloom now. Use a brush to paint individuals with herbicide or dig them out with an asparagus fork before they set seed, prying up as much taproot as possible.

Fertilizer: Spray the garden with an organic fertilizer such as fish emulsion. Some newer brands do not have a fishy smell, but in any case the aroma dispels in a day or two.

Herbs: Most culinary herbs are perennials and can be moved outdoors now in their pots, or planted in the garden after spending a week outside in a sheltered spot to harden off. Because most need good drainage, these are well suited for containers placed in a sunny spot near the kitchen door. Don't fertilize them; most like lean soil. The foremost exception is basil, which should be planted in rich soil at the end of May.

Inchworms: Homeowners can treat very young caterpillars with organic B.t. Or you can have your trees sprayed by a state certified arborist with Conserve, Bulls-Eye BioInsecticide, or Monterey Garden Spray, products that will not harm the environment and that will kill both older and younger inchworms that are feeding. Two applications spaced seven to fourteen days apart will have the best results. For larger kinds of inchworms such as gypsy moths that don't disappear by mid-June, use Pyrethrum, a natural spray with low toxicity.

Lawn reseeding: Last chance to reseed or over seed the lawn until September, which is a much better time to do it anyway.

Perennials: Divide and replant crowded summer and fall bloomers such as Shasta daisy, astilbe, rudbeckia, coreopsis, sedum, aster and chrysanthemum. But wait until fall to divide spring-blooming plants.

Shrubs and trees: Don't overlook flowering trees and shrubs as a source for bouquets. Remove the most neglected or poorest quality woody plants in the garden. For an objective opinion, invite a gardening friend to visit and share opinions on candidates for removal. But don't prematurely remove evergreens that turned brown this winter.

Vegetables: Start melons and cucumber seeds indoors. Plant out seedlings of kale, lettuce, collard greens and other frost-resistant vegetables. Plant the seedlings on an overcast day at the same level they were growing in the trays (not deeper), disturbing roots as little as possible. Then firm the soil around them gently and water to help connect the roots to the surrounding soil. Water newly planted vegetables daily the first week, then twice a week unless it rains. Thin beets, turnips and other seedlings when they get overcrowded and use extras in salads.

Above photos, left to right:

Forsythia

Rhododendron

Tulip

Daffodils

(Boston Globe photos/ John Tlumacki, Janet Knott, Mark Wilson)

Daffodils (Narcissus).

They're the best spring bulb — cheerful, easy and varmint proof. Thousands of cultivars in combinations of yellow, orange, white and apricot are available through mail-order catalogs for fall planting 5 inches deep and 8 inches apart in sun. Try white 'Ice Follies' and yellow 'Carlton.'

(Boston Globe photos/ Mark Wilson, Stan Grossfeld)

HERE COME THE LILACS

EVERY YEAR AROUND MARCH, ONE OF MY WINTER-WEARY NEIGHBORS starts asking me when the lilacs will be in bloom. Well, the wait is over. May is the month when most shrubs bloom, and the lilac is the Queen of the May.

Lilacs' uses are many. Place a garden bench in their shelter for a fragrant bower. Cut flowers for Edwardian-looking bouquets. Plant bushes 3 to 4 feet apart for a shaped or sheared hedge, 4 to 6 feet apart for a flowering screen. Lilacs are among the first bushes to leaf out in the spring and hide the neighbors, and among the last to lose their leaves in the fall.

Left: Old-fashioned lilacs scent the air, complemented by a skirt of equally old-fashioned bleeding hearts. (Boston Globe photo/ John Tlumacki)

Lilacs are hardy in every corner of New England, and few plants have such a strong sentimental association with our region, though in fact they don't much care for acid rain and grow better in more alkaline Midwestern soil.

When colonists arrived with roots and seeds from Europe for their subsistence gardens in New England, the lilac was reportedly the only purely decorative plant they made room for on their ships. It was probably its perfume that won it a place in steerage, for settlers who lived in unsanitary conditions and believed in the healing powers of floral scents were much more appreciative of fragrant plants than modern gardeners.

Syringa vulgaris, the common purple lilac, is the scent of nostalgia, perfuming antique farmsteads and country roadsides, tough relics from an older New England that has all but vanished. There are lilacs believed to have been planted in the 1750s that still bloom on the Governor Wentworth estate in Portsmouth, N.H.

The cult of lilacs reached its peak during the Victorian age.

"You were everywhere," 19th century Massachusetts poet Amy Lowell wrote of lilacs. "You tapped the window...And ran along the road...You stood by pasture-bars to give the cows good milking."

When my own farmhouse was built 175 years ago, it was typically barren of any ornamental plantings except for four lilacs that were set one at each corner of the building, as much a part of its essential architecture as its Greek Revival columns. Today three of them survive, now as large as multi-trunked trees, their flower clusters hoisted skyward a good 12 feet.

Most New England lilacs more than 150 years old are Syringa vulgaris like these: tall, coarse, tough, purple, mildew-prone and richly scented.

Gradually, 22 other species of wild lilacs were brought here, mostly from Asia, providing a variety of colors, forms and bloom times. Syringa oblata is already in bloom, while Prestonia lilacs should flower in June.

The cult of lilacs reached its peak during the Victorian age, when the famous French nursery of Lemoine produced hundreds of named varieties in shades of blue, violet, pink, magenta and white as well as purple, says Jack Alexander, the chief plant propagator at the Arnold Arboretum in Jamaica Plain, MA. Alexander is a third-generation lilac specialist.

Many of these varieties can be seen at Arnold Arboretum, which holds the city's oldest outdoor flower festival, Lilac Sunday, when the 300 kinds of lilacs in its collection reach their peak. Crab apples, dogwoods, redbuds, azaleas, bleeding hearts, creeping phlox and many other plants will

Right: Lilacs hark back to an earlier time when flowers were prized for their scent as much as for their appearance. (Boston Globe photo/ Michele McDonald)

be in bloom, making it the most floriferous weekend of the year to visit the Arboretum.

The University of New Hampshire in Durham also has a nationally famous lilac collection.

One of the attractions of lilacs is that they are almost carefree. Although leaves are often disfigured in humid summers by powdery mildew, it's not a serious problem that requires spraying, and there are many resistant varieties. Otherwise, they're rarely troubled by pests or diseases, though they don't tolerate air pollution well.

Pruning out suckers and a quarter of the oldest branches each year after flowering will help get old overgrown lilacs back to eye (and nose) level, but some gardeners - and I'm one - prefer the tree-like effect of the rugged unpruned trunks of old lilacs. Many of the modern hybrids are shorter. Removing spent flower clusters is unnecessary but is probably the best thing you can do to promote more bloom the following year. An annual top-dressing of compost or an all-purpose tree and shrub fertilizer is also beneficial. Scattering a handful of lime around the shrubs when you lime your lawn is also a good idea.

I do have lilacs that manage to bloom in heavy shade, but the best site is in full sun. Planting on a hillside or a raised bed will promote good drainage. Dig a hole 18 inches deep and 3 feet across and fill it with rotted manure, compost or good soil.

The important thing is to get a new lilac off to a good start. If you plant it well, it can live for centuries. ❈

PICKING LILACS

With so many excellent hybrids available, it makes sense to seek out the best ones for planting at home.

SYRINGA PATULA 'MISS KIM' is a compact, late-flowering, fragrant lilac that has gained popularity for small yards. Unlike most lilacs, it has leaves that turn an attractive mahogany in autumn.

The Arnold Arboretum has selected the following varieties in its collection for their intense fragrance, disease resistance, flower qualit y and landscape form:

BLUE: 'Laurentian,' **'President Lincoln.'**
PURPLE: 'Adelaide Dunbar,' 'President Roosevelt,' 'Assessippi,' 'Excel.'
PALE CREAMY YELLOW: 'Primrose.'
MAGENTA: 'Charles Joly,' 'Ruhm von Horstenstein.'
PINK: 'Catinat,' 'General Sherman,' 'Katherine Havemeyer,' 'Vauban.'

S. X. Chinensis 'Lilac Sundays'

(Boston Globe photos/ Lane Turner)

**Lilacs. S. Vulgaris
'President Lincoln'**

**Lilacs. S. Vulgaris
'Krasavitsa Moskvy'**

Bok choy

Bitter melon

ROOTED IN FOREIGN LANDS

YOU CAN TRAVEL IN YOUR BACKYARD BY PLANTING AN INTERNATIONAL COOK'S GARDEN. Many Asian, South American, and African vegetables and herbs are no more difficult to grow than commonly available vegetables. Some are cross cultural, such as cilantro, which is used in Latin, Indian, Chinese and Middle Eastern cooking.

Cilantro is among the many ethnic plants that have already crossed over into the mainstream. Chili peppers and the so-called yard-long Chinese green beans (or asparagus beans) are in supermarkets now and chayote squash is sold at organic supermarkets.

Jilo (Solanum gilo) is another cross-cultural vegetable, savored in parts of Brazil, where it was brought with the slave trade, and in its native West Africa, where it is known as "garden eggs."

Not all ethnic seeds are commercially available because of a long tradition of taking the seeds from the ripe vegetables themselves, which breed true if they haven't cross pollinated. You can do the same by purchasing ripe vegetables from ethnic markets and using their seeds.

Ajidulce

LEMONGRASS
Grown in: Southeast Asia.
Similar to: Nothing.
Cultivation: Purchase a fresh green lemongrass stalk from an Asian food store in May and stick the root end in water on a sunny window ledge for three weeks. Plant it outdoors when it forms roots. This also works for Thai basil.

BITTER MELON
Also bitter goard, karela, kho-qua, ampalaya, balsamina, Momordica charantia.
Grown in: Asia, Spanish Caribbean.
Similar to: Nothing, though related to gourds.
Cultivation: Direct seed in early June and train on trellises and fencing. Harvest when the fruit is 6 inches long.

AMARANTH
Also Chinese spinach, Joseph's coat, callaloo, quelite, chaulai, pirum.
Grown in: Africa, Asia, the Caribbean, Latin America.
Similar to: Spinach.
Cultivation: Direct seed outdoors in early June; thin seedlings to 6 inches apart. Pinch terminal buds to encourage branching.

AJIDULCE
(Pronounced a-HEE dool-say.)
Grown in: Puerto Rico, Dominican Republic.
Similar to: Bell pepper.
Cultivation: Start seeds indoors in early April for transplanting outdoors a foot apart in early June. Buy mature peppers in a bodega (Latino grocery store) for seed saving. When they're red, the seeds are viable.

CHINESE BROCCOLI

Also gai lan, cai ro, kat na, Brassica oleracea.
Grown in: Asia.
Similar to: Broccoli.
Cultivation: Direct seed from early May through July. Thin to 9 inches apart. Harvest when stalks are 8 inches tall and two or three flowers have opened. Auxiliary shoots will provide additional harvests.

BOK CHOY

Also pak choi, pak-choy, ming choi, Brassica rapa.
Grown in: Asia.
Similar to: Cabbage.
Cultivation: Sow seeds outdoors April through August, 1/4 inch deep and 1 inch apart. Thin seedlings to 6 inches by harvesting the extras for salads when 3 inches tall. Use row covers. Pick only the tender inner leaves and hearts before flowers appear.

Amaranth

Lemongrass

DAIKON

Grown in: Japan.
Similar to: Radish.
Cultivation: Direct seed outdoors in late April.

RECAO

(Pronounced ray-COW.) Also Culantro, Ngo gai.
Grown in: Southeast Asia, Caribbean.
Similar to: Cilantro.
Cultivation: Start the seeds now. Plant seeds or seedlings outdoors in early June in part shade. Can also be grown indoors as a houseplant.

QUIABO

Grown in: Africa, Latin America.
Similar to: Okra.
Cultivation: Start seeds in April in peat pots and plant outdoors in early June, 18 inches apart. In July, start harvesting young pods every other day to keep them producing.

CALABAZA

(Pronounced ca-la-BA-sa.)
Grown in: Central and South America, Caribbean.
Similar to: Butternut squash.
Cultivation: Plant seeds indoors in April and seedlings or seeds outdoors in early June, with three plants or seeds planted an inch deep and 4 inches apart on 6-inch-high hills of soil spaced 4 feet apart. ✿

(Boston Globe photos/ Lane Turner)

GARDENER'S WEEK 1

Deer repellents: Those containing the fungicide Thiram seem to work best. Spray tulips and other plants at risk. Sources include Deerbusters (301-694-6072; www.deerbusters.com).

Lawn grubs: You can tell if they are a problem by tugging at dead grass patches. A tuft that pulls out easily usually has had its roots devoured by grubs. But it takes strong poisons to kill them this late in their life cycle. It's better to wait and apply controls in mid-July. The best low-impact chemical control for grubs is the pesticide Imidacloprid.

Lead concentration in soil: It can be dangerously high for growing edibles in some urban vegetable plots and those located near old buildings where lead paint long ago flaked off. Visit www.umass.edu/plsoils/soiltest.html to find out about soil testing, or send a stamped, self-addressed envelope to Soil Testing, UMass Extension, French Hall, 230 Stockbridge Road, Amherst, MA 01003.

Planting: You can plant all shrubs, trees and perennials. But wait for late May to set out tender annuals.

Weeds: Get them before they bloom. One year's seeding equals seven years' weeding. Perennial weeds spread by stolons or rhizomes such as witch grass can be weeded now that the newly sprouted roots have used almost all their energy and are vulnerable.

TOP 10

Herbs. These are a cinch to grow:

10 **Bee balm (Monarda didyma).** The flowers are edible as garnishes, or can be dried for potpourris.

9 **Dill (Anethum graveolens).** An annual that doesn't like to be transplanted, so sow seeds in a sunny place.

8 **Mint (Mentha).** Most kinds are easy and vigorous enough to plant in sunken containers to keep them from spreading aggressively.

7 **Lavender (Lavandula angustifolia).** The purple flowers can be eaten, but most people grow this for fragrant bouquets and potpourris.

6 **Lemon balm (Melissa officinalis).** Use the intensely lemon-scented leaves as an insect repellant, furniture polish or salad ingredient.

5 **Marjoram (Origanum majorana).** This most delicious variety must be treated as an annual in New England, preferably grown in a pot that's never allowed to dry out.

4 **Sage (Salvia officinalis).** The common culinary variety. It needs full sun and good drainage, and prefers a raised bed or pot to grow in.

3 **Thyme (Thymus vulgaris).** This highly valued culinary thyme is used in a bouquet garni. Plant it in a sunny spot with good drainage.

2 **Chives (Allium schoenoprasum).** This may be the easiest of all herbs, and is free of pests and diseases.

1 **Basil (Ocimum basilicum).** It needs watering and attracts some pests, but it's well worth the extra effort.

GARDENER'S WEEK 2

Annuals: Sow bachelor's button and nigella seeds outdoors.

Evergreen hedges: Now that hemlocks require expensive spraying for wooly adelgid, people are turning to a new hybrid arborvitae called Thuya x 'Green Giant,' which grows quickly to 20 feet and is deer resistant, though it's not as shade tolerant as hemlocks.

Flowering shrubs: Prune them immediately after they finish flowering to ensure you will not cut off next year's flower buds.

Garlic mustard: This invasive biennial weed is blooming now with small four-petaled white flowers on 1- to 2-foot stalks. The leaves have scalloped edges and smell like garlic when crushed. Seeds remain viable in the soil for years, so continue weeding it out every year until no more appear. Most weeds are harmless and merit only a casual response, but to identify garlic mustard and other seriously invasive plants before they get out of control, visit www.umassgreeninfo.org for photos.

Hostas: This is a good time to plant or divide emerging hostas. Varieties with thick and stiff blue leaves are more resistant to slugs. Compounds containing iron phosphate provide additional slug control.

Lawnmower care: It's time to mow. Don't try to make it look like a putting green. Your lawn will be healthier and shade out most weeds if you keep it at 2 1/2 inches.

Mosquitoes: Dump and remove objects such as old tires that collect water and become breeding grounds for mosquitoes. Use Mosquito Dunks (available at garden centers) to keep them from breeding in water features unless you have fish. They'll eat the larvae.

Perennials: Thin phlox and delphinium plants to five stalks this week or next. Set out stakes before perennials grow too tall, especially if you're using grow-through supports such as metal circular hoops for peonies.

Roses: They should be leafing out now. Cut back all brown, dead canes to live green stems.

Vegetables: Start seeds of squash and pumpkins indoors. Sow parsley seeds outdoors.

KNOW YOUR TERMS

CULTIVAR: The name given to a new plant variety by its original grower, bracketed by single quotes. Example: Sedum 'Autumn Joy.'

Above photos, left to right:

Spring tulips are massed for effect at Boston's Copley Square.

(Boston Globe photo/ David L Ryan)

GARDENER'S WEEK 3

Annuals: Wait until next weekend to buy most annuals. Salvia, nigella, scabiosa, calendula, sweet alyssum, snapdragons, nicotiana, cleome and petunias can be planted now.

Chervil: Anthriscus sylvestris is an invasive weed with white flowers in June that look like Queen Anne's lace on 4-foot stalks with ferny leaves. Mow it now and apply Dicamba (Banvil) next month (at two pounds per acre) or mow low repeatedly to deplete root reserves. It's also susceptible to Roundup sprayed just prior to flowering. Visit http://pss.uvm.edu/vtcrops/ articles/WildChervil.pdf for more information.

Roses: Spray delicate hybrids (but not robust shrub roses) weekly with wettable sulfur fungicide or fungicidal soap through the end of June.

Sunscreen: Always apply it before heading outdoors to garden. And wear a hat.

Spring flowering bulbs: Sprinkle bulb fertilizer around bulbs. Deadhead them but don't pull or cut the foliage until it turns completely yellow, as it's storing food for next year's flowers. Planting annuals around them next week will help disguise the unattractive leaves. Many people remove and discard tulips altogether as they often don't rebloom well. If you choose to pull out your tulip bulbs, you can free up their space for summer annuals and then plant top size new tulip bulbs in October.

Vegetables: Harvest radishes. Cut spinach when the leaves are 7 inches long. Cut the outer leaves from leaf (as opposed to head) types of lettuce. Harvest the top half of mesclun mixes with scissors so they can continue to grow. Pick young red rhubarb stalks by cutting or grabbing the stalk and pulling it upward and slightly to one side. (Don't eat the leaves.) Make another sowing of beets, carrots and lettuce seeds. Wait one or two weeks to transplant tomato, pepper and eggplant seedlings into the garden, but they can be hardened off now by spending more and more hours outdoors each day. Protect beets and Swiss chard from the beet leafminer by covering them with floating row covers of lightweight spun polyester. (Remay is one type.) Also secure this over cabbage, cauliflower and broccoli to protect them from the cabbage root maggot fly. Planting the vegetable garden with herbs such as rosemary, chives, catnip, thyme and mint will discourage some pests.

Above photos, left to right:

Rhododendron

Marigolds

White lilacs

Pansies

Purple Lilacs

Pink dogwoods

(Boston Globe photos/ Pam Berry, Michele McDonald, Lane Turner, Pat Greenhouse, John Tlumacki)

GARDENER'S WEEK 4

Annuals: Shop now for greatest selection. For best results, select plants that have not bloomed yet. Put a few grains of a time-release fertilizer such as Osmacote into each planting hole. Water well after planting and water daily for the first week unless there's rain, and twice a week thereafter.

Beans: This is one of the easiest and most productive vegetables to grow. Plant bush and pole bean seed 2 inches deep a foot apart, and keep planting them every two weeks until September. Keep them picked while they are young so the vines stay productive.

Container gardens: These can be planted now and throughout the summer. Select attractive pots, baskets, urns, boxes and tubs. (Some nurseries will plant these for you.) Containers should have drainage holes or slits in the bottom so that water flows through freely and plants

don't rot and die. Fill containers with a high-quality soil-less mix, which is also called premium or professional potting mix. It consists of peat, vermiculite and shredded bark. Not only is the mix good for plants (oxygen, fertilizer and water reach roots readily), but the light weight makes containers easier to move. Buy one of the new potting mixes with pre-measured time-released fertilizers and water-holding crystals, or add gradual-release fertilizer to the soil before planting. Follow package instructions for amounts.

Herbs: Sow basil, calendula, dill, fennel, summer savory and shiso seeds. Seed cilantro in the garden every two weeks for a continuous harvest of leaves. When the seeds start turning brown, collect them by cutting off the stalk and sticking it facing downward in a paper bag.

Perennials: Cut asters and chrysanthemums back by a third to make them shorter and bushier, and repeat this at the end of June.

Sunflowers: Plant either seeds or young plants 3 feet apart. They do well in poor soil but need full sun.

Tomatoes: Plant them this week or next, 2 inches deeper than they were growing in their pots. Buy young plants no more than 8 inches tall. Don't plant them where they grew last year (in other words, practice crop rotation) or you'll encourage soil-borne diseases. If curly top virus has been a problem in the past, causing stunting, leaf roll, yellow foliage and eventual death, don't plant tomatoes until mid- to late-June to avoid most leaf hopper insects that spread the disease. Keeping the garden weeded and covering tomatoes with a light shade cloth also will help foil this and

other diseases. Check varietal tags. If tomato transplants are marked "Indeterminate" they will continue to grow and produce all season. Plant these 15 inches apart unless they will not be staked, in which case space them 3 feet apart. Varieties marked "Determinate" are usually early varieties that produce their fruit all at once and do not need staking. Plant these 1 to 2 feet apart. Planting basil with them will help repel tomato hornworm.

Vegetables: Hill potatoes by pulling soil up against the plants when they get a foot high, and protect them from Colorado potato beetles with row covers. Plant corn.

Siberian iris (Iris siberica).

These are the easiest irises to grow in New England, and they are elegant in a vase. Most have violet-blue flowers but some are white, yellow, pink or multi-colored and have artful veining. At 3 feet, 'Caesar's Brother' is probably the strongest grower and a heavy bloomer. Pictured at far left is the 'Isabelle,' below middle is 'Velvet Night,' and below right is 'Polly Dodge.'

(Boston Globe photos/ Pam Berry)

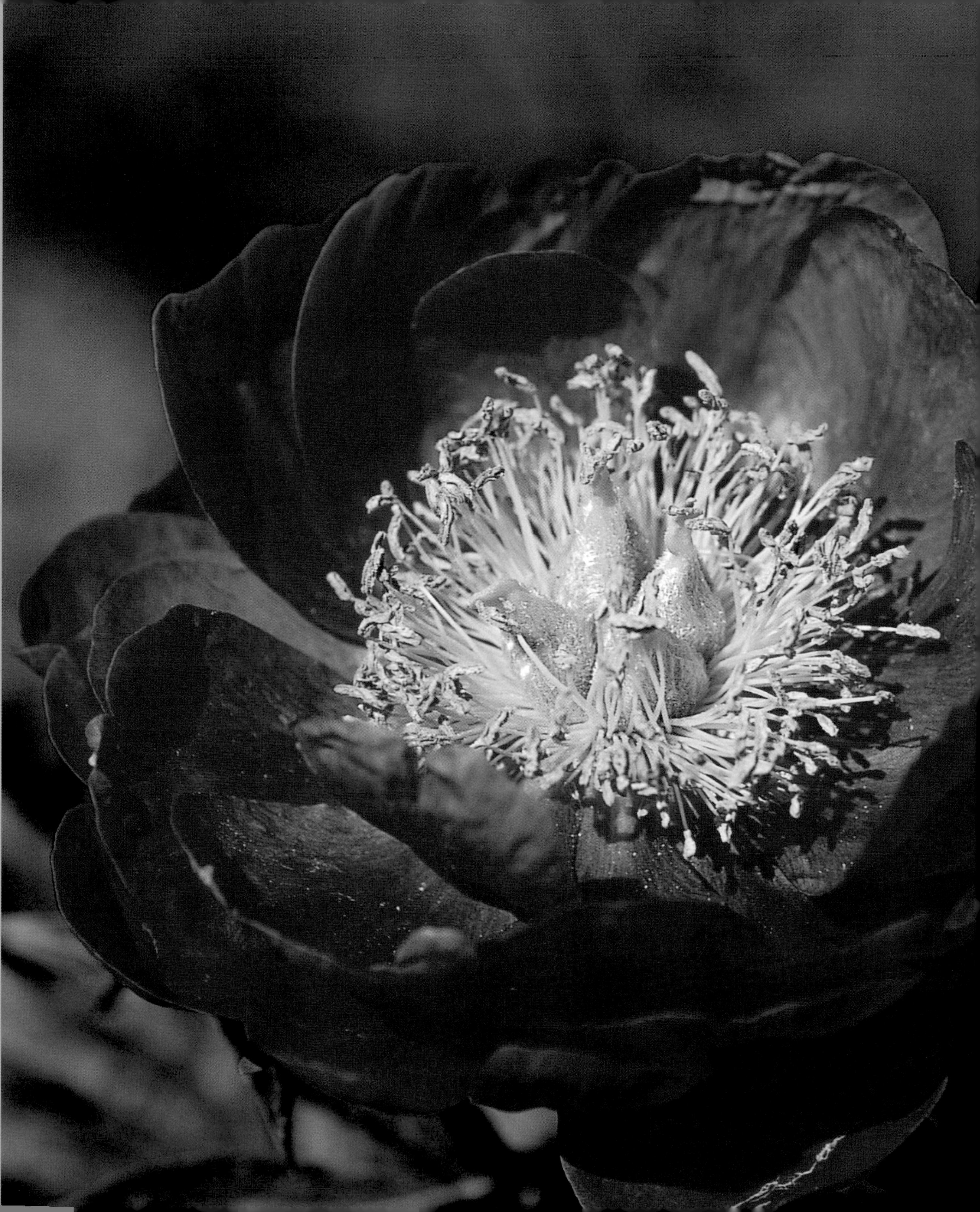

PEONIES ON PARADE

THIS IS THE TIME WHEN WE MOST COVET THE PLANTS BLOOMING IN OTHERS' YARDS.

If you envy your neighbor's gorgeous peonies, plan now to plant some in September.

Don't confuse the opulent perennials we call herbaceous peonies, which die down every winter, with the related shrubs called tree peonies. Herbaceous peonies are what you want to grow. Tree peonies are what you want to avoid. One of the few drawbacks of herbaceous peonies is that they're slow to build up a head of steam. You may have to wait a couple of years to get flowers. But tree peonies are the tortoises of the flower world. They could take a decade to produce any amount of flowers. So forget those.

Left: Paenoia Coral Magic. (Photo courtesy of www.songsparrow.com)

Paeonia 'Lord Calvin'

Paeonia 'Shin Lo'

My favorite herbaceous peony – because it's the best performer of the dozen types I grow – is 'Festiva Maxima,' a fragrant white peony with crimson flecks that was introduced into commerce in 1851 and is still the most popular variety. It's a fragrant, many-petaled double with strong stalks that hold up the flowers in the rain. Many peony stalks break or bend if it rains while they're in full bloom because the flowers are so heavy, so consider getting types with fewer petals – such as Japanese, anemones, semidoubles and singles instead of the ball-like old-fashioned doubles.

But you can't beat the doubles for fragrance.

I grow both and stake them with peony hoops that have been in my husband's family for 60 years. Fifteen years ago we drove 1,000 miles to get his mother's peony

hoops because you could no longer find them in stores and we wanted to replicate her peony hedge. But fortunately, peonies have regained their popularity, so that peony hoops, which are metal circles with legs, are now easy to buy locally.

Good fragrant varieties of double peonies include 'Mrs. Jules Elie,' dark pink 'Wilford Johnson' and double cream 'Lord Calvin' with candy-striped accents.

Good performers that are less fragrant and less full, but also less likely to require staking, include 'Paula Faye' (a semidouble, glowing pink doer in the garden), 'Sparkling Star' (a pink single), 'America' (a dark crimson-red single) and 'Cytherea' (a cup-shaped flower in the new coral color).

Most peonies are easy to grow if you have sunlight. But

Peonies can be red, pink, white or coral, with many petals or just a single row, but they all bloom in June and can live for many decades.

(All photos courtesy of www.songsparrow.com)

Paeonia 'Madylone'

they bloom only for a couple of weeks a year, so if you're looking for fragrant, cutable flowers with a long period of bloom, you're better off with roses.

However, I think a hedge of peonies is especially nice along a narrow strip in full sun next to a driveway because the plants die down in winter, giving you a place to pile shoveled snow. And a mix of varieties is more fun and gives you a longer period of bloom than using just one kind. Mine last three weeks. But the most important consideration is to order plants of the same height, because peonies vary in height from 24 to 36 inches. Klehm's Song Sparrow Farm and Nursery publishes a full-color catalog that gives height as well as color and blooming time of plants. It can be ordered by calling (800) 553-3715 or visiting www.songsparrow.com.

It's always better to plant peonies in the fall, though you can plant them now if you buy them in pots. Don't use any fertilizer and make sure not to plant the base of the stems, or "eyes," more than 2 inches deep or they'll never bloom. (If you have peonies in a sunny spot and after three years they're still not blooming, they may be planted too deep.) Scratch a handful of bonemeal in around each plant in the fall, but never right after planting. Throw a few evergreen boughs or a winter mulch on new peonies in December, to be removed in March.

And incidentally, the ants you often find around peony buds are harmless. Wish we could say the same thing about the deer! ✤

How Does Your Garden Glow?

YOU ALWAYS PICTURED YOURSELF IN A BRILLIANTLY COLORED GARDEN bathed in sunlight. But now the image strikes you as ironic because you're away at the office all day, you're on the go all weekend, and the time you're most apt to spend in your yard is the twilight hour after work.

If you and your yard seldom meet in broad daylight, a romantic moon garden designed for evening viewing makes surprising sense.

When you think night, think white. I used to consider white gardens effete and boring. My mind was changed by my discovery (while weeding in rapidly fading light) that every garden has both a daytime and a nighttime personality. White flowers that look merely pleasant by day become luminous at night.

The eye perceives colors differently in low light. Reds and blues retreat while yellows, light pastels, and especially whites glow because of their ability to reflect even scarce light. Those red red roses and celestial blue delphiniums that dominate the garden by day have all the charm of black holes at night. But take another look at that white sweet alyssum edging. Unassuming by daylight, it becomes as dramatic as surging surf when the sun is setting.

After a hectic day at the office, it helps quiet me down to watch the garden make its evening transition from multicolor to monochrome as bright colors fade to gray and white flowers assume their lunar glow.

White gardens are traditionally called "moon gardens" because they were designed to be viewed by moonlight. The moon, of course, generates no light of its own and is only reflecting the sun's light. The white flowers of the moon garden take this illusion one step further, reflecting a reflection.

Some white flowers don't even have any pigmentation of their own, and are really as colorless as water. They look white because, like snow, they are filled with air spaces which reflect even scarcest light. Try squeezing the air

Above: Sanguinaria canadensis (double bloodroot) blooms in April. The flowers look like miniature water lilies and get their name from the orange sap that bleeds from broken roots. (Photo courtesy of New England Wild Flower Society/ Dorothy Long) Right, clockwise: Scaevola, rose form impatiens, begonias, hibiscus. (Photos courtesy of Proven Winners® – www.provenwinners.com)

CHOOSING A MOON GARDEN

Here are some suggestions for choice and mostly fragrant moon garden flowers, as well as sources for the plants and for more information about them:

• **The best-performing white annuals in hot summer weather which you are apt to find as starts now in local garden centers include cleome or spider flowers, sweet alyssums, nicotiana hybrids such as 'White Nicki,' ageratums, garden geraniums, cosmos, petunias, verbenas and zinnias for sunny sites. Impatiens, lobelias and pansies are good for shade. Most are not fragrant and all come in various shades so ask for white flowers and don't settle for mixed colors.**

• **The new garden phlox 'David' is a top perennial that has a lovely scent and blooms from July to September if seedheads are removed. Most perennial nurseries carry it.**

• **Perhaps the easiest perennial for the shady moon garden is a hosta with white variegated leaves such as Hosta decorata, or one with white fragrant flowers, such as Hosta plantaginea, which blooms in August. 'Honeybells' is a hybrid that has fragrant lavender flowers in July and white edging on the leaves.**

• **There are a number of flowers that release their perfume specifically at night to attract pollinating moths. If you grow annuals from seed, consider sowing moonflower vine (Ipomosa alba), night-scented stock (Matthiola bicornis) or old-fashioned white-flowering tobacco (Nicotiana sylvestris or the less fragrant N. alata grandiflora) for their rare evening fragrance next spring.**

• **Plants with very pale silver leaves such as annual dusty miller and many of the perennial artemesias and lamb's ears also show up well at night. Consider fall blooming pearly everlasting (anaphalis triplinervis) and June flowering edelweiss to do double duty, since they have both white flowers and silver foliage. Some are carried by White Flower Farm at 800-503-9624 or www.whiteflowerfarm.com.**

• **"Alba: The Book of White Flowers" by Deni Brown (Timber Press) is an English gardening book filled with ideas for the white garden. It has information on how to grow 1,000 white-flowered plants, though not all are hardy on this side of the Atlantic.**

pockets from such a white petal and it will turn colorless.

Author Vita Sackville-West's white garden at Sissinghurst in England is a famous moon garden, as is the one in Litchfield, CT, from which the nursery White Flower Farm takes its name. (The original plan of the first owners was to sell only white flowers, but the appeal proved too limited.)

Some old Victorian gardens actually feature "moongates" with circular openings designed to frame the rising moon on special nights, an idea borrowed from Asia.

But these days there are many effective ways of supplementing moonlight. Since one of the most effective plants for the evening yard is the fragrant white moonflower vine, Maine landscape designer Barbara Damrosch suggests incorporating some kind of lamppost into the scheme as a luminous focal point and support for this moth-pollinated climber. Her book "Theme Gardens" (Workman Publishing) contains an easy plan for a moon garden that would bloom spring through fall.

I prefer white in a summer garden because that's when people spend time outdoors at night, so I concentrate my own selection of white flowers on warm weather bloomers and don't bother with white daffodils or mums.

You can create your moon garden by putting a small special bed of white flowers around an outdoor patio. But I just add a lot of white summer annuals to my main garden after Memorial Day. When they're killed off by frost in October, brilliant mums and asters are already kicking in for a more colorful fall garden.

For immediate gratification, your best bet is to pick up some of the many common white-flowered annuals available at local garden centers. These mass-marketed plants are not apt to have much scent, but there are many less commercial white plants that can make the moon garden an especially fragrant place.

Butterflies don't care much for white flowers, but moths prefer them, so some white flowers such as sweet rocket and Nictoiana sylvestris attract them by emitting a strong scent, like perfumed soap, at night.

You may already have a moon garden and not know it. I discovered a self-sown stand of wild pink and white sweet rocket in a corner of my yard which is inconspicuous by day but emits a delicate clove-like scent from gleaming petals at night. Once you have sweet rocket, it will always spring up somewhere in your yard.

Though moths are the counterparts to butterflies in the moon garden, nothing tops fireflies for adding a magical touch. If you want to encourage them, leave a corner of tall grass unmowed in your yard where they can breed. If you're lucky, your garden will generate its own source of light. ❀

Right: A birdbath provides a low-key accent amid giant alliums, peonies, lady's mantle, perennial geraniums and nepeta 'Six Hills Giant' in Carol Stocker's front yard. (Boston Globe photo/ Pam Berry)

GARDENER'S WEEK 3

Annuals: After annuals planted in the garden exhibit fresh growth, circle each plant with a tablespoon of 10-10-10 granular fertilizer, being careful not to let it come in direct contact with the plants, which can be burned by the salts it contains. Then water. Alternatively, spray the young plants' leaves and stems with a water-soluble fertilizer. This is better for annuals growing in pots or window boxes.

Green manure: Plant buckwheat in empty beds to increase soil fertility.

Lawns: Don't let the grass grow too long between mowings so you can leave the cuttings on the lawn as fertilizer. The most important reason to have a mulching mower is to be able to chop fallen leaves finely enough that they can remain in the lawn to feed earthworms and beneficial soil microbes that reduce compaction, provide nutrients, and improve drainage.

Also, you can feed your lawn by raking 1/8 inch of peat moss or compost over it to build up its organic content.

Lilies: They're beautiful, but resist buying them or you'll have to spray them every two weeks to protect them from the new and voracious red lily leaf beetle. Buy daylilies instead.

Peonies: Cut or snap off spent peony blossoms but leave the stalk. If left on the bush, moldering flower heads can promote botryis blight. Remove any stalks or leaves that turn black from this blight before it spreads to the rest of the plant.

Roses: Cut flowers just above an outward-facing leaflet, and then cut the stems again under running water just before arranging. If you have not yet fertilized your roses, do so now.

Slugs: Watering in the morning instead of the evening can reduce slug damage to plant leaves such as hostas.

Tomatoes: Growing tomatoes in cages is a good compromise between staking and sprawling. Tomato cages can be purchased, or made by rolling and fastening a 6- by 4-foot roll of concrete reinforcing wire mesh into a 22-inch-wide cylinder.

Vegetables: Sow more carrots. Harvest them when they're between 1 and 2 inches in diameter. Gently pull out some delicious young "new" potatoes when the plants start to flower. Leave the plant intact to produce mature potatoes, which will be ready when the tops have withered.

GARDENER'S WEEK 4

Annuals: There's still time to grow many annuals from seed, including agrostemma, bupleurum, calendula, celosia, centaurea, coreopsis, cosmos, gypsophila, gomphrena, ornamental kale, larkspur, marigold, morning glory, nasturtium, nigella, phlox and reseda.

Edging: If you're hosting the annual July 4 barbecue in your yard and don't have much time to tidy up, forget about weeding. Instead, just edge the beds for a neat, fresh appearance.

Houseplants: Keep houseplants you moved outdoors out of direct sun, and check to see if they need water daily in hot weather by lifting them. Dry pots will be lighter.

Garden structures: Inspect and repair trellises, stone walls and other structures and consider adding improvements.

Lawn: Plan on covering high-traffic areas with pavers or decking so you don't have to deal with dying grass in compacted soil.

Meadows: To keep them looking neat, discourage invasive plants and control infant trees and shrubs, mow them once now and a second time in late fall.

Peas: Harvest snow peas before the peas begin to fill the pod. Pick snap peas anytime, as the pods remain edible at any stage. English peas are ready to harvest when the pods are bright green and the peas start swelling inside. If the pod is dull green and the peas have passed their prime, harvest them anyway to keep the vine producing.

Perennials: Stake floppy perennials. Shear the tops of spring bloomers such as candytuft, gold dust, rock cress and moss phlox with grass shears after flowering to ensure a uniform and ornamental foliage effect for the remainder of the season. Dig, divide, and replant overcrowded bearded iris soon after they finish blooming. They don't keep blooming well unless they are divided and replanted every five years. Discard any soft or diseased rhizomes and replant them horizontally so the roots hang down and the tops are parallel with the surface of the soil. This is the last week to pinch chrysanthemum and shear back asters for more compact and floriferous late-fall bloom.

Tomatoes: Keep soil evenly moist and don't apply too much nitrogen, which can cause poor fruit set. Water early in the day so plants can dry out quickly. Cut off suckers.

Vegetables: Fertilize them once a month.

Roses (Rosa).

No plant can compete with roses for fragrance, variety and length of bloom. I prefer the newer low-maintenance "landscape roses" such as pink 'Bonica' and 'Carefree Beauty' and the climbers 'Dortmund' (left) and 'William Bafflin,' all long blooming, very disease resistant and winter hardy. Hundreds of roses bloom sequestered by hedges in the James P. Kelleher Rose Garden in Boston's Fenway (above).

(Boston Globe photos/ Pam Berry, Janet Knott)

FUN WHILE THEY LAST

IF YOUR GARDEN SEEMS PREDICTABLE, ADD SOME FAST FLASH WITH TROPICAL PLANTS. When people enter your backyard to find the giant, colored leaves of cannas and bananas, you'll instantly overturn any ho-hum expectations.

The last time tropical plants were this popular was a century ago, when estates had greenhouses and gardeners to tend them. Tropical plants were rare status symbols then. Now they're cheap and widely available.

Massachusetts garden designer Kevin Doyle admired the Australian tree ferns at the Wellesley College greenhouses for years and even ordered one that was only 4 inches tall when it arrived from an expensive specialty company. Then one day at the indoor plant section of a Home Depot, Doyle beheld 19 tree ferns. They were 4 feet tall and $19.99 each. He bought all of them. "I was in heaven. Someone later asked me, 'Where did you get those? They must have cost hundreds of dollars!' So I said, 'Yes, they did.' "

Left: Palms prefer a hot, sunny site with well-drained soil and protection from wind. (Boston Globe photo/ Janet Knott)

By definition, tropical plants are not winter hardy. Most depart this world with the first touch of frost, meaning that unless you move them indoors for the winter, they are one-season wonders. But consumers interested in unusual annuals have become more willing to pay for disposable plants. So breeders for big companies such as Ball Seeds have dived into the tropical gene pool in search of a new plant material.

Now, many tropicals have been hybridized into high-performance annuals and the collector's item of yesterday is available at the local garden center today. This is especially true of salvias and coleus, once despised but now prized, thanks to the many new kinds on the market. The cannas and dahlias, so beloved by Victorians, are also enjoying a comeback thanks to breeders' magic. Many new ones have leaves as colorful as their flowers. As gardeners have rediscovered these old-time favorites, appetites have been whetted for experimenting with much more exotic summer bulbs, such as flowering ginger-lily.

So if you are ready to risk flamboyance, here are 10 terrific tropicals worth trying:

BANANA PLANT

(Musa, Ensete)
Origin: Asia.

Description: Treelike, with large, paddle-shaped leaves and usually inedible fruits, they provide vertical accents. Wind resistance makes them good for balconies.

Care: Grow in full sun. Cut them back hard before frost and winter them in the basement for larger plants next year.

Also consider: Musa sumatrano 'Zebina Rojo' has handsome striped leaves, grows 10 inches in 12 weeks, eventually reaching 3 to 5 feet in containers, larger if planted in the ground.

CANNA

Origin: Central and South America.

Description: These fast-growing, narrow, banana-like plants reach 6 feet in one season for a vertical accent or temporary hedge, planted 18 inches apart. There are also dwarf varieties.

Care: Grow them in rich soil in full sun for bright flowers, or part shade for foliage, which is often colorful. Potted canna can also be immersed in garden ponds. Grow them as annuals or cut off the tops after frost and store rhizomes indoors in peat moss at around 50 degrees for replanting the following June. You can also store the roots in pots of soil kept dry.

Above: Large, boldly colored and patterned foliage (such as this Elephant Ear) is more important than the flowers most tropicals produce. (Photo courtesy of www.parkseed.com)

Right: Grow canna in rich soil. (Boston Globe photo/ Janet Knott)

Above: Formal decorative dahlias have perfect symmetry. Right: Papyrus like boggy conditions and can add a tall vertical accent to a garden pond. (Boston Globe photos/ Matthew J. Lee, Janet Knott)

COLEUS

(Plectranthus scutellarioides hybrids, Solenostemon)

Origin: Southern China to northern Australia.

Description: These are grown for their many colorful leaf combinations as annuals or houseplants. Size varies from 1 to 3 feet tall; there are many spectacular new varieties.

Care: They are easy to grow in sun or shade. You can winter over prized varieties as houseplants or by taking several 5-inch cuttings from the parent plants and putting them in a glass of water until roots grow and are ready for planting.

DAHLIA

Origin: Cool mountainous regions of Mexico, Central America and Colombia.

Description: Diverse, showy, large hybrid flowers shaped like daisies, balls, or water lilies come in every color but true blue. Use them for containers, borders or cutting, depending on the height of the variety, which can range from 1 to 6 feet. Look for the types with maroon leaves for extra pizzazz.

Care: Grow in full sun. Stake taller varieties. After fall frost, they can be discarded as annuals, or the tubers dug and stored over the winter for May replanting.

HIBISCUS

Origin: Worldwide; varieties such as Kosteletzkya, Hibiscus moscheutos, H.syriacus and rose of Sharon are winter-hardy here.

Description: There are 300 species of perennials, annuals, shrubs and trees for gardens, large containers and flowering hedges. All have many large hollyhock-like blooms in assorted colors lasting a single day each.

Care: Choose easy, old-fashioned species instead of fussier hybrids. Grow them in full sun.

HEDYCHIUM

(Ginger-Lily, Butterfly Ginger)

Origin: Southeast Asia and Indonesia.

Description: These narrow, 4- to 8-foot reedy, stemmed plants have sweetly fragrant yellow, white, scarlet, pink or orange flowers that bloom periodically through the summer in sun or half shade when watered thoroughly.

Care: Buy potted plants to grow in filtered light in rich soil with plenty of moisture. To winter over, cut off the canes and dig up the rhizomes before the first frost. Store these roots in peat moss and replant in June, after cutting rhizomes into sections with a sharp knife, leaving at least two red protruding "eyes" on each piece.

PALMS

(Brahea, Butia, Chamaerops, Jubaea, Nannorrhops, Phoenix, Trachycarpus and many others)

Origin: Warm regions around the world, including South America and the Mediterranean.

Description: Their strong foliage adds a variety of exotic architectural shapes to gardens.

Care: Most prefer a hot, sunny site with well-drained soil and protection from wind. If you want to winter them inside, grow them in pots.

PAPYRUS

(Cyperus)

Origin: Africa and Asia.

Description: These grass-like annuals and perennials may grow to 6 feet in boggy conditions and make good accents to garden ponds.

Care: Plant in a very moist site in sun or part shade. They can winter over as odd-looking houseplants.

PLECTRANTHUS

(Swedish ivy)

Origin: Australia, Asia and Africa.

Description: This diverse container annual is grown for its ornamental, textured leaves and fall spikes of tubular blue flowers.

Care: Easy and fast-growing in sun or shade.

SALVIA

Origin: Widely distributed.

Description: This group includes more than 750 species of annual, biennial and perennial plants for hot, dry, sunny locations. Colorful 2-foot spikes of purple, blue, red, pink or white flowers attract hummingbirds and butterflies. Non-hardy Salvia greggii, including the Simply Beautiful 'Navajo' series, has novel bloom colors, while S. guaranitica has intriguing dark blue flowers with black sepals.

Care: Easy and drought resistant in full sun, they often rebloom if you cut back spent flowers.

Right: Kevin Doyle is adept at designing with tropical plants, but here he gets a tropical effect in his own Dover, MA, garden using winter-hardy perennials with bold foliage, such as cimicifugas and hostas. (Boston Globe photo/ Janet Knott)

NATURE'S SUMMER CONCERTS

TURN OFF THE AIR CONDITIONING AND OPEN YOUR WINDOWS: there's a concert going on in your backyard. Insects are some of the world's finest musicians, and millions of them are doing now what birds do in the spring: They're singing to claim territories and mates.

As with birds, the performers are mainly male, but instead of raising their voices, most musical insects rapidly rub their wings or legs together. Some perform by day, particularly the meadow insects that can hide in tall grass. The greatest variety, though, play at night, when they have fewer predators. After all, a noisy insect is deliberately attracting attention to itself, so why do this when the bird population is up and hunting for breakfast?

It can be difficult "to tell the oboes from the clarinets" in the orchestra, says Chris Leahy, author of the "Insects" guide in the Peterson First Guides series published by Houghton Mifflin. He adds that when he has led evening field trips for the Massachusetts Audubon Society, "people are amazed by how many different sounds there are."

The greatest variety is in slightly wooded neighborhoods with terrain that can include ponds and wetlands. Still, Leahy says you can hear night insects (which tend to be in trees and shrubbery) almost anywhere except the busiest city centers where traffic drowns them out.

"You can have crickets in your urban apartment building or even your kitchen driving you crazy at 3 a.m. They'll survive on food debris, even newspaper and cardboard," says Roger LeBrun, professor of entomology at the University of Rhode Island.

In China, people consider it good luck to have a cricket as a pet. They keep crickets in cages, some quite elaborate, and bring them to parks for singing contests.

The northern field cricket begins chirping in New England as early as April, but the main concert begins in July and continues through October. Insects hatch in the spring and must finish growing up before they have mature wings to play on, and an interest in mating.

The familiar, cheerful chirp of the northern fall field cricket is the easiest insect sound to recognize, but there are other kinds performing now, too. Six species of small ground crickets produce various high tinkling trills that collectively meld into what Leahy describes as the shimmering sound of summer.

Snowy tree crickets are Leahy's favorite insect musicians. With their translucent wings, "they are as close to being living ghosts as you can get," he said. "They look like spun glass."

They're also called the thermometer cricket: Take the number of chirps in 13 seconds and add 40 to get the outdoor temperature in Fahrenheit. The call of the snowy tree cricket, a loud, repeated singsong that sounds like "ka-zink," is actually an alternating duet in stereo. One male produces the first syllable, and another responds with the second syllable in a kind of call-and-response pattern. Nathaniel Hawthorne wrote, "If moonlight could be heard, it would sound like that."

The northern true katydids also respond to one another's calls, though their rasping choruses are less musical. Leahy likens the katydid sound to Darth Vader whipping his light sword around with a snap of syncopation.

These bright green katydids are some of the noisiest "stridulating" insects, the ones that rub their wings together.

Far left and below: Cicadas all hatch at once by cracking open the hard shell of their adolescent exoskeletons to emerge with wings on their back and a tympanum in their abdomen that they can vibrate to make quite a racket. (Photos courtesy of Robert D. Childs, UMass Amherst; and Massachusetts Audubon Society)

Left: Bright green katydids rub their wings to call to each other. (Photo courtesy of Massachusetts Audubon Society)

The sound of a tree-top colony of jamming katydids can be so loud that people call the Massachusetts Audubon Society every year, hold their phone to the window, and ask, "What's this?"

Familiar meadow grasshoppers add a papery, short rasp to the summer orchestra, which provides an undertone to the crickets and katydids. Also in the background is a common meadow musician called a conehead, which Leahy says produces a rapid pulse of lisps at the rate of about 10 per second.

Summer's little musicians don't seem to be decreasing in numbers.

Cicadas are very different from the other singing insects and don't rub their wings together. "Instead, they have a mechanism in their abdomen," says Leahy. "It's like if you take a Coke can and press the top and get a clinking sound. Cicada vibrate this tympanum at a high rate of speed."

Most cicadas are tree dwellers. The common one is called the dog days cicada because you hear it at the height of summer. While many of the other musical insects magnify volume by creating a resonating chamber with their wings, cicadas, as loud as katydids, use an internal air sack.

Summer's little musicians don't seem to be decreasing in numbers. In fact, they're quite abundant, and birds are among their biggest fans. Some types live in trees, some in bushes, and some in grass.

Obviously, insects are more apt to perform nightly in your yard if you don't use pesticides. Leahy also suggests leaving a patch of grass unmowed.

These insects are herbivores, but Leahy doesn't consider crickets and their kin particularly destructive. Still, "tree crickets inject their eggs in tree branches," he acknowledges, so "a large number might kill a branch."

The musical tempo is dictated by temperature because the insects' metabolism rises with warmth. It will continue into autumn at a slackening pace.

"One of the subtle melancholy touches of fall," Leahy writes in an issue of the Massachusetts Audubon Society journal Sanctuary, "is the progressive slowing of the night concert until, one especially frosty November evening, the last fiddler falls silent."

To hear the sounds of night insects, visit www.findsounds.com and type in "grasshopper," "cicada," "conehead," "katydid" or "cricket" at the prompt. Also, visit http://buzz.ifas.ufl.edu. ❀

GARDENER'S WEEK 1

Annuals: Fertilize them every three weeks. Some gardeners prefer an organic 8-8-8 fertilizer or half-strength Peter's Super Blossom Booster, which is high in phosphorous to promote blooming rather than leaf growth. Give container plantings a weak dose of liquid fertilizer every three weeks.

Compost: Turn compost pile.

Fragrant herbs: Scented geraniums come in a large variety of fragrances but aren't winter hardy, so pot these up so you can bring them indoors in the winter. Their leaves are used in potpourri. Chamomile and heliotrope are other top choices. If you want to try to grow lavender, which doesn't like our acid soil, plant it in potting soil mixed with a little lime in a container. Harvest the floral spikes while they're still in the bud stage. Some other fragrant herbs are invasive and

should also be contained in pots; these include bergamot and the many kinds of mint (pineapple, spearmint, peppermint) and easily reseeding lemon balm, which can all also be used to flavor herbal teas and other drinks. For information on joining The Herb Society of America, call 440-256-0514 or visit www.herbsociety.org.

Perennials: Spray garden phlox, roses and monardas with a solution of one tablespoon baking soda to a gallon of water to prevent white powdery mildew on leaves. Spray hollyhocks with sulfur to prevent rust spots on leaves.

Rhododendrons: If you want to deadhead these, be careful not to remove the new shoots on either side of the old flower head. If you find C-shaped notches along the edge of leaves, you have black vine weevils. These night feeders can be trapped

by loosely wrapping a piece of burlap around the base of the shrub. The weevils will hide there by day and can be removed.

Silver foliage: If you worry about flower colors clashing in the garden, don't use white flowers as the peacemaker. They are too dominant and will upstage everything else. Silver foliage plants such as annual dusty miller and Dichondra 'Silver Falls' or perennial artemisia are the answer.

Watering: If it rains less than an inch per week, water enough to make up the difference. How can you tell how much rain has fallen? Buy a rain gauge or check the daily tally of recent rainfall in your local newspaper.

White grubs: Apply Merit this month to areas of lawn where white grubs have been a problem. To check their presence, turn over a square foot of sod and look for C-shaped tiny white grubs with dark heads. More than 10 per square foot constitutes a problem. Commercial nematode products usually don't do the job (but work well in container gardens). Milky spore disease doesn't work well in the New England climate, either.

Above photos, from left to right:

Tiger swallowtail butterfly on astilbe flower

Apricot begonia

Magenta echinacea

(Boston Globe photos/ John Tlumacki, Pam Berry)

GARDENER'S WEEK 2

elphiniums: To get the ngest flowering time from ese plants requires some mplicated pruning. Cut back e big impressive flower stalks ter they've finished blooming encourage the small side anches to flower. When they're ne, cut off the spent blooms t let the leaves remain until ey start to look ratly and w leaves and stems sprout m the base. Then cut the old ems to the ground. With good nditions, the new shoots will ntinue to grow and eventually om modestly in the fall. elphiniums are heavy feeders at rarely live more than two or ree years.

uit: Pick blueberries in the orning and don't wash them til you use them.

Perennials: Remove any diseased leaves or plants as soon as you spot them. Prune or thin established perennials to keep them in their desired space, especially if they're overtaking and shading annuals and perennials planted earlier this year. Cut back pest-infested, yellowing or declining foliage on columbines, hollyhocks, daylilies, tall bearded iris, geraniums and other plants. Most will produce clean new growth, even if they don't rebloom. Divide bearded iris.

Row covers: Remove them when temperatures reach 80 degrees to avoid damaging plants with overheating. Remember that it will be warmer under the cover.

Tomatoes: Mulching helps protect your plants from being splashed by fungus spores in the ground when it rains. It also suppresses weeds and conserves water.

Vacation: You may have plans to take off, but who's going to water the plants? Most plants need to be hydrated twice a week in the summer. If you can hire someone or enlist a helpful neighbor, leave detailed instructions for watering houseplants, which can be easily drowned. (It's rare to over-water plants growing in the ground.) How long plants survive without watering depends on what you're growing and how hot (or rainy) the weather is. Gardens can usually go two weeks without watering, while plants in pots thrive for only one week. Container gardens will do better if you move them to a shady location where they are standing on mulch or soil, not on stone or concrete that can conduct heat. It will also help if you can dig holes and bury the containers up to their rims. There are also gel packets on the market that can be left on top of potted plants to slowly release water for 30 days.

Vegetables: Thin overcrowded seedlings by snipping them off at the base with scissors. Sow seeds of lettuce, Chinese cabbage, beets, beans, rutabaga, turnip, kale, collards and cabbage directly into the garden for a fall crop. Pick cucumbers before the skins get tough and they turn yellow. Harvest broccoli when the buds are about to open, cutting the top 6 inches of stem. Side branches will continue to produce for two more months.

KNOW YOUR TERMS

GRAFTING: The practice of fusing one type of plant onto another. Most roses of desirable varieties are grafted onto the more vigorous roots of an inferior variety. The bulge in the trunk where the two varieties have been joined is called the "graft."

GARDENER'S WEEK 3

Annuals: Don't let your annuals go to seed. Most need you to remove their dead flowers to keep them producing new ones. First you have to learn to tell flower buds, which are soft and squishy, from seed heads, which can look similar (especially in the case of pansies) but are harder to the touch. Each species is different. For instance, petunias bloom at the tips of their stems so you must pinch off the seed heads along the length of the stems without cutting the stems themselves. This is done more easily with your thumb and forefinger than with snippers. Deadheading can be a time-consuming business, but you can quickly shear back small flowered plants such as pansies and sweet alyssum by collecting all the stems together in one hand and cutting off the spent flowers all at once with clippers in the other hand. If you don't want to deadhead, you can grow colorful foliage plants like coleus, or impatiens or the new 'Profusion' strain of zinnias, which is slow to go to seed. Another tactic is just to keep cutting flowers for bouquets.

Aphids: To keep your aphid population down, blast them off desirable plants with a hose. They can't climb back on. You can also encourage wild Queen Anne's lace, which attracts tiny wasps, and marigolds, which draw hover flies. Both insects kill aphids by injecting their eggs into them.

Perennials: Spring and fall is when most of the work needs to be done. Summer is for enjoying your beautiful garden. So keep planting, transplanting and dividing to a minimum until the end of August. Water established perennials after they've been without rain for two weeks, but water first-year plantings every week. Prune sprawling perennials to keep them in their space and remove any disease- or insect-plagued foliage.

Pesticides: U.S. homes apply 80 million pounds of pesticides each year, some of which have been linked to serious health problems. In Massachusetts, the website www.kellysolutions.com/ma can help you search for legally registered pesticide products for every potential pest. Just plug in the pest you want to control, the product name or the active ingredient. Another website, www.extremelygreen.com/pestcontrolguide.cfm, lists strictly organic solutions for insect problems.

Vegetables: Harvest green peppers at any size when you have an immediate use for them, as they don't store well. Left on the vine, they'll turn red like hot peppers but keep their mild flavor. Harvest eggplant when they reach 4 inches and are still shiny. Harvest garlic when the top four to six leaves have started to brown. Dry them, braid the leaves together and hang your "garlic garland" in an airy place.

Above photos, from left to right:

Tomatoes

Ruby-throated hummingbird

Magenta impatiens

Massed beds of colorful annuals, including red geraniums, yellow marigolds and pink begonias

(Tomatoes photo courtesy of W. Atlee Burpee & Co.; Boston Globe photos/ John Tlumacki, Pam Berry)

GARDENER'S WEEK 4

Biennials: If you allow sweet Williams, foxgloves, hollyhocks and forget-me-nots to go to seed now, their offspring will flower for you next year, though the parents will die. These plants are called biennials because their lifecycle takes two years – one year to sprout from seed, and a second year to flower, set seed and die. Hollyhocks will survive longer if after they flower you cut them back to the new foliage at the base (basal foliage) instead of letting them go to seed. Though Alcea rosea is the common multicolored hollyhock species, look for yellow flowered Alcea rugosa, which is longer lived, more disease-resistant and doesn't need staking.

Lawn mowing: Let your grass grow to 3 inches in July and August. A taller lawn doesn't need as much water, helps shade out weeds and encourages more beneficial insects to keep the soil healthy. Mowing higher also produces deeper grass roots. Try not to remove more than a third of the top growth at one time.

Oriental bittersweet: Keep an eye out for tall, questing shoots of this invasive Asian vine sprouting in your garden and reaching out for something to clamber over. Birds spread the decorative orange fall berries, so it can pop up anywhere. Once established, Celastrus orbiculatus, as it's known in botanical Latin, spreads rapidly and is very hard to remove. So don't let it get a foothold. You can recognize it by its teardrop-shaped leaves that taper to a point, and its orange roots.

Trees: Remember to water newly planted trees weekly, along with those that have been defoliated by inch worms. This includes municipal street trees in front of your home. Most tree roots are shallow but they extend up to five times the width of the canopy, so water over a large area.

GREAT GARDENS TO VISIT

Maine

JOHNNY'S SELECTED SEEDS TRIAL GARDENS
Foss Hill Road
Albion
www.johnnyseeds.com
207-861-3900

THUYA LODGE GARDEN / ASTICOU TERRACES
Rte. 3
Northeast Harbor
Mount Desert Island
www.asticou.com/gardens.html
800-258-3373

Massachusetts

BERKSHIRE BOTANICAL GARDENS
5 West Stockbridge Road
Rte. 102 and 183, Stockbridge
www.berkshirebotanical.org
413-298-3926

TOWER HILL BOTANIC GARDEN
11 French Drive
Boylston
www.towerhillbg.org
508-869-6111

New Hampshire

THE BALSAMS
Rte. 26
Dixville Notch
www.thebalsams.com
603-255-3400

FULLER GARDENS
10 Willow Ave
North Hampton
www.ohwy.com/nh/f/fullgard.htm
603-964-5414

Rhode Island

BLITHEWOLD MANSION AND GARDENS
101 Ferry Road
Rte. 114, Bristol
www.blithewold.org
401-253-2707

GREEN ANIMALS TOPIARY GARDEN
Cory's Lane
Portsmouth
www.newportmansions.org
401-847-1000

Butterfly weed (Asclepias tuberosa).

This is a choice native milkweed for full sun, with glowing, translucent orange buds that open into bright flowers irresistible to butterflies. In the fall it produces a different kind of show, with silver milkweed pods that release their seeds on silken parachutes.

(Photos courtesy of Massachusetts Audubon Society, left, and www.parkseed.com, below)

AUGUST

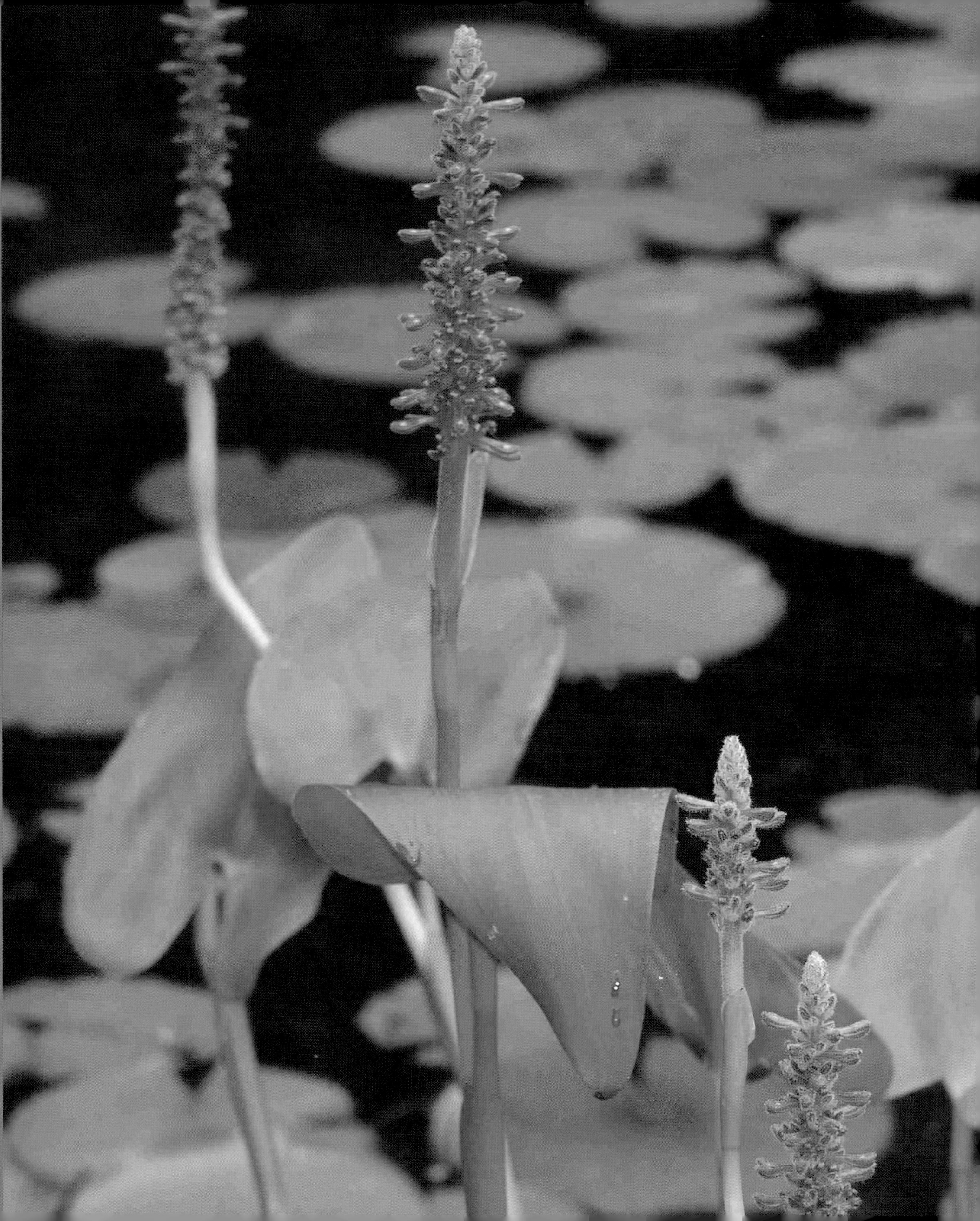

THE WATER GARDEN OASIS

EVERY SUNDAY MORNING, MEMBERS OF THE SHARRY FAMILY hang out with bagels and the newspaper on the banks of their garden pond. It's only 100 feet from their 1813 Massachusetts farmhouse, but the spot feels secluded. "You have to walk down a garden path. It's relaxing and pretty," says Jack Sharry. "Our kids just watch the frogs. Our landscape designer, Kevin Doyle, cemented a rock to the bottom so they can step out into the pond. A big family of frogs showed up the first day the water was put in."

Maybe they heard that water gardening has become one of the fastest-growing areas in landscaping.

When it comes to commercially installed water gardens, the sky's the limit. But now that high-quality, flexible liners have come down in price, it's also possible for do-it-yourselfers to build a backyard pond for as little as $1,000.

Left: Bog plants such as this Sagittaria 'Arrowhead' thrive in shallow pond areas. (Photo courtesy of New England Wild Flower Society/ Jeff Carmichael)

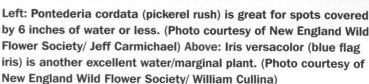

Left: Pontederia cordata (pickerel rush) is great for spots covered by 6 inches of water or less. (Photo courtesy of New England Wild Flower Society/ Jeff Carmichael) Above: Iris versacolor (blue flag iris) is another excellent water/marginal plant. (Photo courtesy of New England Wild Flower Society/ William Cullina)

"Everyone wants a water feature," says Doyle. "It brings you one level closer to leaving the harried world when you get home. It's primal."

Water gardens have a lot to offer, including the opportunity to grow new plants and build an aquatic ecosystem that attracts birds, frogs and dragonflies. But the soothing sound of moving water is the biggest attraction.

"I want to hear it. And I don't want it to sound like a leaky faucet. I want it to be musical," says Doyle. He likes to use an oversized water pump that has a spigot that shoots water. He installs it underwater so the jet breaks the surface by several inches. "It makes a foaming gurgle, almost like opening a big keg of beer. It's a very soothing swish. The aerating water is always white and the pond is always black, so it has a visual effect, too."

"The sound of the water is definitely the biggest thing because it creates tranquility," agrees Andre Golden, head of sales for New England's largest aquatic nursery – Paradise Water Gardens in Whitman, MA. "People install fountains, waterfalls and statuary spitting water in the pond. Waterfalls are the biggest trend right now. You get a lot more sound out of a waterfall. They're not hard or expensive to do. Just mound up soil at one end of the pool and cover it with liner. You can use the same pump for the filter and for the waterfall."

Moving water also provides oxygen for fish that eat mosquito larva. "Most people aren't putting in still-water ponds, especially with the mosquito issue," says Golden.

One major expense can be installing backyard electricity to run the pumps. For in-line voltage, plan on installing it 18 inches underground to pass electrical inspection. All cabling, connections and fittings for pumps attached to the main electrical supply should be safety approved for outdoor use. The voltage lines should be installed by a qualified electrician. The system must be protected by a circuit breaker and a ground fault interrupter.

Lighting extends the hours of enjoyment and redefines the pond at night. Underwater lighting is most atmospheric, but don't light the entire pond and leave it on all night, or you'll disturb the fish. You can buy and install inexpensive, low-voltage systems that reduce the current through a transformer but are powerful enough to light a small pool.

Water gardening can become addictive. "Most people end up rebuilding their pond two or three times because they started too small," warns Golden. "A good size is 15 feet by 15 feet. It's going to start acting like a natural pond and take care of itself."

The key plants for a healthy aquatic ecology are those with completely submerged leaves, such as hornwort and anacharis, which provide oxygen to the fish and control algae. Floating plants such as water lilies also help control algae growth by shading the water.

Lotus is the most spectacular of the flowering water plants and is hardy in much of southern New England. But it's invasive and difficult to control. Paradise Gardens devotes an entire pond to lotus, but for a mixed garden, water lilies are a better choice.

It's easier to winter-over aquatic plants and fish in in-ground ponds than in raised ones. "The plants have no problem, they can freeze up solid and come back," says Golden.

Fish need a little more help. In addition to a minimum depth of 18 inches, they require an inexpensive heater to keep a hole in the ice so methane gas can escape. (Don't try chipping a hole in the ice yourself. Shock waves from cracking the ice can kill the fish.)

Golden likes to buy small koi, which cost about $10 for a 5-inch fish. "They're very colorful and long lived and they eventually grow large."

Doyle prefers to go to pet shops on goldfish rescue missions. "There's always a tank of little gold fish they call 'feeders' for the piranas. I feel like the ASPCA because I buy a dozen feeders and I'm giving them a break. They're usually 99 cents for 10."

In either case, the frogs usually materialize for free. ✺

CREATE A GARDEN POND

It's possible for two people to install a 15,000-gallon pond (approximately 12 feet in diameter) for about $1,000 in three weekends. Here's how:

SELECT A SITE

It should be sunny. Most water lilies need at least six hours of direct sunlight a day. Stay away from trees, or you'll be digging through roots. Have a nearby electric outlet, as you'll need an electric pump.

Put the pond near outdoor seating, or plan to put seating near the pond, so you can enjoy the sound of the water. Another possibility is by the front door, where the pond can serve as a welcoming feature.

CHOOSE A MEDIUM

The two least-expensive pond options for do-it-yourselfers are preformed plastic and vinyl liners. Preformed plastic is confined to ponds 8 feet in diameter or smaller. Before you start digging, move a preformed plastic pond around the garden until you find a spot you like. If you're planning a flexible vinyl liner, outline the proposed location with a garden hose and mark it with a trail of lime or flour. Plastic liners should be about 45 mils thick and come with a 20-year guarantee.

BEFORE THE BIG DIG

Check with local utilities before you start digging (call 800-DIG-SAFE) to ensure that you don't run into in-ground power, water or sewage lines, and check with your municipality for any legal restrictions, such as fencing that might be required around ponds of a certain size. Also, don't forget to review the plan for your own in-ground irrigation or sprinkler system, if you have one, so you don't accidentally destroy it. Check your homeowner's insurance policy to see if it has restrictions against a pond like the one you're planning and whether a pond is covered.

DIG IT

This is the most difficult part. It will go more easily if you soak the soil deeply with water and then rototill the next day to break it up. Remember, you have to excavate only about 18 inches deep. Any deeper and you have a swimming pool, not a garden feature, and you'll definitely have to fence it. Any shallower and fish won't survive the winter.

Dig out the soil to about an inch less than the depth of a preformed pond, which should sit a little higher than the surroundings.

Add 2 inches of sand at the bottom or put down an old carpet or an inch of old newspapers to help protect vinyl liners from perforation. None of this is necessary for preformed or molded ponds, but make sure there are no sharp objects such as roots or rocks in the hole.

INSTALL THE POND

Put the liner in the hole. Make sure top edges are level by laying a board across the pond and placing a carpenter's level on top. Don't walk inside the liner with shoes on.

Fill the pond one-third full with water, and pack the space outside the liner with sand or excavated dirt. Continue filling with water while backfilling around the outside. The water level should always be slightly above the level of the backfill during this process to guarantee that the pond walls are fully expanded. This is the trickiest part of installing a preformed pond, back filling while you are adding water, so the mold doesn't buckle. Tamp the soil down firmly as you go, checking continuously with a carpenter's level. If it's not level, have someone pull up on the edge of the pond while you tamp fill underneath.

DECORATION

Use flat stones to create a decorative edge and conceal the top of the liner or the lip of the preformed pond. This also protects it from the ultraviolet rays in sunlight, which can damage the plastic.

ACCESSORIES

Install a 110-volt outdoor electrical outlet with a ground-fault circuit interrupter (or have one installed) to run the pump. The size of the pump you'll need is determined by the size of the pond. It will run 24 hours a day.

Install a filtration system to keep the water clean. The pump will circulate the water through the filter. Both the pump and filtration system should be selected according to the volume of water in the pond. For a 1,500-gallon pond, you'll need a 1,500-gallon filter and a 4,280-GPH (gallons per hour) pump.

FINALLY, THE PLANTS

Select water plants that are winter hardy, and adopt some goldfish. Plan on one submerged potted plant and an inch of goldfish for every square foot of pond surface. Some plants are free floating, such as water lettuce and water hyacinths; others, such as water lilies, are rooted in underwater containers with a few rocks on top to keep them on the bottom. Put bog plants such as blue flag iris, Japanese iris, cattails, arrowhead and pickerel rush in the shallow parts of the pond, where they will be covered with 6 inches of water or less.

SMART WATERING

WATERING BECOMES THE NUMBER ONE CONCERN of good gardeners during the hot summer months.

If your city or town has not enacted water restrictions, give everything a long deep drink, especially shrubs and trees. This includes the city trees on the sidewalk strip in front of your house, though you don't technically own them. (Lack of watering, not pollution, is the biggest killer of young street trees.)

Take your sprinklers and start circulating them around your yard, setting them in each spot for about three hours.

The best time to water is in the morning.

It takes me about a week to cover my entire yard once. Then I start over again. The goal is one inch of water applied once a week.

The best time to water is the morning, when the sun will dry leaves to prevent fungus growth without evaporating most of the moisture you're delivering to the soil.

Most people water wrong. They turn on a hose or sprinkler system for a few minutes several times a week, wetting only the top of the ground and encouraging shallow roots that get scorched by the heat near the soil's surface when that water evaporates.

Drought-resistant plants have deep roots. To get roots to go deep, you need to get the water down deep, too.

There, insulated from heat by a few inches of soil, water can be stored in the ground. Think of watering as refilling the reservoir of moisture in the soil, rather than wetting its surface. It doesn't matter if the top of the ground is wet or dry. What's important is that when you stick your finger an inch deep in the soil, it's moist down below.

TUNA CAN METHOD

The low-tech way to ensure this is called the "tuna can method." Put an (empty!) tuna can under your sprinkler and keep watering until it's full.

If you see runoff, you're watering faster than the ground can absorb. Leave that spot for a while and then come back to it.

How do you prioritize if you can't water everything? The answer is counterintuitive. Let your lawn go brown, but keep watering your trees.

The lawn that isn't watered looks like it's dying, but it isn't. It's just going dormant and will revive in the fall, when rain and cooler temperatures arrive.

But valuable trees that aren't watered will look OK, when in fact they could die. It works like this: Trees stressed by drought will soldier on, perhaps only losing their leaves earlier in the fall without much color change. Leaves just go from green to brown instead of red and gold, and the tourists are put out.

Often the effects of drought will not be felt until next year, when the weakened trees start to succumb to pests and diseases they would otherwise have been able to fight off. Watering is especially vital to trees fighting off pandemics, such as dogwoods and many kinds of maples.

If your community has a watering ban and only allows, for instance, hand watering with a hose or watering can, your triage becomes more ruthless. My favorite tool for hand watering is a Walkman and a book-on-tape, because you have to stand there a long time to do deep watering over a large area with a hose. Keep the nozzle moving so that the water has a chance to sink in without runoff; water only in the mornings and evenings, when less water evaporates.

MILK JUG STRATEGY

If you're reduced to using a watering can, take plastic gallon milk jugs, cut off the bottoms and punch small holes into the sides. Then dig them upside down into the ground next to your most precious plants, like your tomatoes, and fill them with water that will slowly leak into the soil depths you're trying to reach.

Plants growing in containers are exceptions to the once-a-week watering rule, as their roots experience evaporation on all sides. They need daily watering with a watering can or hose. Polymers such as Water Grabber that are soaked in water and then mixed with your potting soil will reduce watering chores.

Finally, lay off the fertilizers. Plants stressed by drought don't need chemicals forcing them to put out extra growth, any more than someone suffering heatstroke needs to be entered in a marathon. In hot weather, fertilizer can act more like a poison pill than a vitamin. ❀

Left: A Daphne x burkwoodii 'Carol Mackie' takes a drink. Think of watering as refilling the reservoir of moisture in the soil rather than wetting its surface. (Boston Globe photo/ Pam Berry)

Above: Long-blooming, heat-loving, drought-resistant and cheerful in bouquets, black-eyed Susans are the perfect summer perennial. (Boston Globe photo/ Matthew J. Lee)

Above: Garden phlox are fussier, requiring thinning, frequent watering and deadheading. (Boston Globe photo/ Matthew J. Lee)

GARDENER'S WEEK 1

Annuals: If you haven't had time to pinch off individual spent blossoms, shear back tender and half-hardy perennials such as petunias, verbenas, snapdragons and portulacas by one-third to one-half when they stop blooming. Then apply a water-soluble fertilizer to promote a second wave of flowers before summer's end.

Container gardens: Water daily in hot weather. Your outdoor container plantings are especially vulnerable to dehydration because moisture evaporates on all sides of the pots and the roots are confined to a small area. To ensure air circulation, pots should be placed at least 3 inches apart in groupings. Terra cotta pot "feet" or small pieces of wood under each pot will also help air circulation. It's better not to put outdoor pots in saucers because the standing water can cause root rot.

Corn: Don't harvest corn before the kernels burst with milky juice when pierced. This happens when the silks at the end of the ears turn dry and brown, usually about three weeks after they first appear.

Fall-blooming bulbs: Order and plant colchicums and autumn crocus now.

Fertilizer: Continue to feed annuals and potted plants, but stop fertilizing perennials for the rest of the year to allow plants to begin to prepare for winter.

Insect pests: Don't use pest lures that attract everyone else's pests to your yard. The worst are those "bug zappers" that attract flying insects to fluorescent and ultraviolet light and electrocute them. Since they don't discriminate between "good" and "bad" insects, they can also wipe gardener's friends such as green lacewings.

Perennials: Cut back tired-looking plants that have finished blooming to make room for late-bloomers. Remove any sun-scorched or diseased foliage.

Shrubs: Don't prune shrubs until they lose their leaves this fall or you may encourage the growth of new stems that don't have time to prepare for winter.

Summer squash: You can eat these at any size, but they taste best when relatively small and when the skin is still glossy.

Tomatoes: Don't remove leaves that shade fruit or they can suffer sunscald.

Watering: Be vigilant about providing an inch of water once a week to garden flowers, vegetables, trees and new plantings. To reduce losses to evaporation, water early in the day or use a soaker hose. Both techniques also help avoid fungal plant diseases.

Above photos, left to right:

Corn field

Annual pink cosmos

Corn on the cob

Blue delphiniums

Dill

(Boston Globe photos/ John Bohn, John Tlumacki, Wendy Maeda, Pam Berry; dill photo courtesy of www.parkseed.com)

GARDENER'S WEEK 2

All-America Selection gardens: You can see next year's new flower and vegetable varieties on trial all season at the Massachusetts Horticultural Society gardens, 900 Washington St., Wellesley; the UMass Amherst Durfee Conservatory, Newton Centre Green at Centre and Beacon streets; the Berkshire Botanical Garden at 5 West Stockbridge Road, Stockbridge; and the University of New Hampshire trial garden at Prescott Park, Marcy Street, Portsmouth, NH. Visit www.all-americaselections.org for more information.

Hanging baskets: They can be difficult to water unless you have a good long-handled "watering wand." Once the soil has dried hard, water runs over the surface and down along the planter sides without fully soaking the thirsty roots. If this happens, take the plant down from its hook and immerse the entire pot and roots in a bucket of water until it fully rehydrates. Hanging baskets can

require watering both morning and evening in hot weather.

Roses: To minimize black spot, water roses early in the day and try not to wet their leaves. Apply a fungicide if you see black spots surrounded by yellow rims on the leaves.

Tomatoes: Fluctuations between dry spells and soakings make them more prone to pests, cracking and diseases, so water regularly twice a week early in the day, being careful not to wet the foliage.

Trees: It's most important to keep them watered, but roots need air as well. To aid large trees struggling in New England's typical heavy clay soil, use an auger to create 18-inch-deep holes scattered through the root zone.

Vegetables: Sow seeds of beets, chard, spinach and lettuce for a fall harvest. Monitor cabbage, broccoli, cauliflower and Brussels sprouts for cabbage worm and cabbage looper. If any are found, pick them off or spray with Bacillus thuringiensis (B.t.).

Watering: Leave the irrigation system, sprinkler or soaker hose on for at least two hours once a week where water is needed. A light spritzing can do more harm than good as roots grow to the top of the soil to capture any water that comes its way, making them more vulnerable to heat. A 2- or 3-inch layer of bark or some other kind of organic mulch will conserve moisture and reduce watering needs.

GREAT GARDENS TO VISIT

Vermont

BURLINGTON BOATHOUSE
College Street, Burlington
www.onjoyburlington.com/boat-house.cfm; 802-865-3377

SHELBURNE MUSEUM
Rt. 7, Shelburne
www.shelburnemuseum.org
802-985-3346

Connecticut

CAPRILANDS HERB FARM
534 Silver St., Coventry
www.caprilands.com
860-742-7244

ELIZABETH PARK ROSE GARDEN
150 Walbridge Road
West Hartford
www.elizabethpark.org
860-231-9443

GARDENER'S WEEK 3

Cover crops: Plant vacant areas such as harvested sections of the vegetable garden with a "green manure" of annual oats. Because it will be killed by winter, flipping the roots upside down and working the vegetative matter into the layer of soil below ("turning under") this cover crop next spring can be done with a garden fork. It is much easier than turning under winter hardy cover crops such as winter rye or winter wheat, which require a tiller. But plant these if you wait until early- to mid-September to sow, which is too late for oats. All these cover crops will help prevent weeds, erosion and leaching while adding organic matter to the soil.

Dill and fennel: Harvest the leaves anytime. Cut stalks and put them upside down in a paper bag to harvest the seeds as they turn brown.

Hydrangeas: The most winter-hardy common types all have white flowers. They are Hydrangea arborescens 'Annabelle,' H. paniculata (Pee Gee) and H. quericifolia (oakleaf). Blue-flowered varieties often loose their flower buds to winter damage, so try the newer blue variety 'Endless Summer,' which produces buds in the spring. Watering blue-flowered hydrangeas with a gallon of water mixed with an ounce of aluminum sulfate can encourage deeper blue flowers in colored hydrangeas, but will not change the color of white ones.

Invasive plants: Many of the top 20 offenders are common landscape plants that jump the garden fence and take over conservation land. Don't buy Norway maple, bishop's weed, Japanese barberry (even varieties with colored leaves), burning bush, yellow flag iris (Iris pseudacorus), Japanese honeysuckle, shrub-like honeysuckles (Lonicera morrowii, L. x bella, L. Maackii, L. tartarica or L. japonica) or purple loosestrife (Lythrum). Remove any you already have, especially if you live near wild areas or open land. For information on environmentally friendly substitutes, visit the New England Wild Flower Society website at www.newenglandwildflower.org.

Lawns: They usually need help during late summer in the form of one or two deep irrigations to maintain vigor and to give them a good start into the fall season of prime growth. Fertilizing lawns in the heat of late summer is a bad idea.

Perennials for cutting: The best for bouquets now include perovskia, helenium, lobelia, hosta, balloon flower, knautia, garden phlox, globe thistle, sea holly, yarrow, black-eyed Susan, coneflower and heliopsis. 'Becky' is the best white Shasta daisy variety. Plant some of these this fall for more cut flowers next summer. Bouquet material to grow in partial shade includes aruncus, monkshood, astrantia and astilbe.

Vegetables: Harvest shallots and onions when their leaves are half browned. Let these bulbs dry in the sun for a day or two, then cure them by storing them in a dry and well-ventilated spot for another week. Harvest scallions when the bulbs are less than an inch across and bunching onion, which are under-developed green onions, at any time, and use them without drying. Hill soil up around leeks to produce long white stems and harvest them in the fall. Continue sowing autumn crops such as mustard greens, Savoy and Chinese cabbages, beets, escarole, kale, radishes, collards, kohlrabi, lettuce, parsnip, peas, radicchio, salsify, spinach and turnips. Row covers will help them grow faster.

GARDENER'S WEEK 4

Lawns: Now through early September is the best time to reseed existing lawns to rejuvenate them and smother weed growth. Once the grass seed is planted, water it thoroughly and keep the lawn watered to help the seed germinate.

Lyme disease: The most effective protection against Lyme disease, which is carried by black-legged deer ticks that hang out in tall grass (not lawns), is using repellents when in tick-rich areas and dressing preventively, which means wearing light-colored pants tucked into light socks so these tiny black ticks are easier to spot on your clothes. Do a "tick check" before you come inside.

Peonies: Peonies resent transplanting and don't need division, so don't dig up established clumps unless you must because, for instance, trees have grown up around these long-lived plants and are shading them. Plant peonies by digging a hole 2 feet across and 1 1/2 feet deep and mixing the soil with one-third peat moss or leaf mold, two handfuls of bone meal and a handful of lime. Shallow planting depth is the crucial thing. Buds must be positioned only 1 to 2 inches below the soil surface or they'll never bloom. Fill the hole two-thirds with soil, then fill it with water. After it's drained, set the unpotted plant in the hole. It helps to lay a stick across the opening so you can gauge soil level accurately. If the plant is too low, remove it, gradually fill in more soil, and set the plant in the hole. Keep doing this until the tops of the pink buds or the base of the stems are less than one inch from the stick, as it may settle slightly lower. After planting, water to firm down the soil (but don't step on it).

Trees: Rake up leaves of apple, pear, crabapple and hawthorn trees, which have probably fallen because they're infected with apple scab disease, which can winter over on fallen leaves. Trees that are already showing significant fall color or losing their leaves this early in the year may be stressed by drought or over fertilizing. If they were planted in recent years, check that they were not planted too deeply. If the area where the trunk meets the top of the roots, descriptively called the "root flare," is buried, excavate around it to expose it to air. Never pile up mulch against tree trunks or you'll cover up this root flare.

Vegetables: Plant seedlings of Chinese cabbage and seeds of radishes, spinach, Swiss chard and lettuce for a fall harvest. Harvest okra when the pods are no more than 3 inches long and keep them picked frequently so production continues.

Weeding: Weeds have to be pulled before they set seed. Roots cling less tenaciously to damp soil, so weed after a rain or after irrigating. Deep tap roots such as dock, pokeweed and dandelion can be pried out of the ground with a long slender fishtail weeder or grubbing knife. Do not compost weed seeds.

Above photos, left to right:

Pee Gee hydrangeas

Foxgloves

Hanging verbenas

(Boston Globe photos/ Janet Knott, Pam Berry; verbenas photo courtesy of Proven Winners® – www.provenwinners. com)

Zinnias (Zinnia).
These sun-worshiping easy annuals bloom in bright terracotta shades that spell summer. I like the large flamboyant strains such as 'State Fair,' which I cut frequently for long-lasting bouquets. This only encourages the plants produce more flowers.

(Photos courtesy of www.parkseed.com)

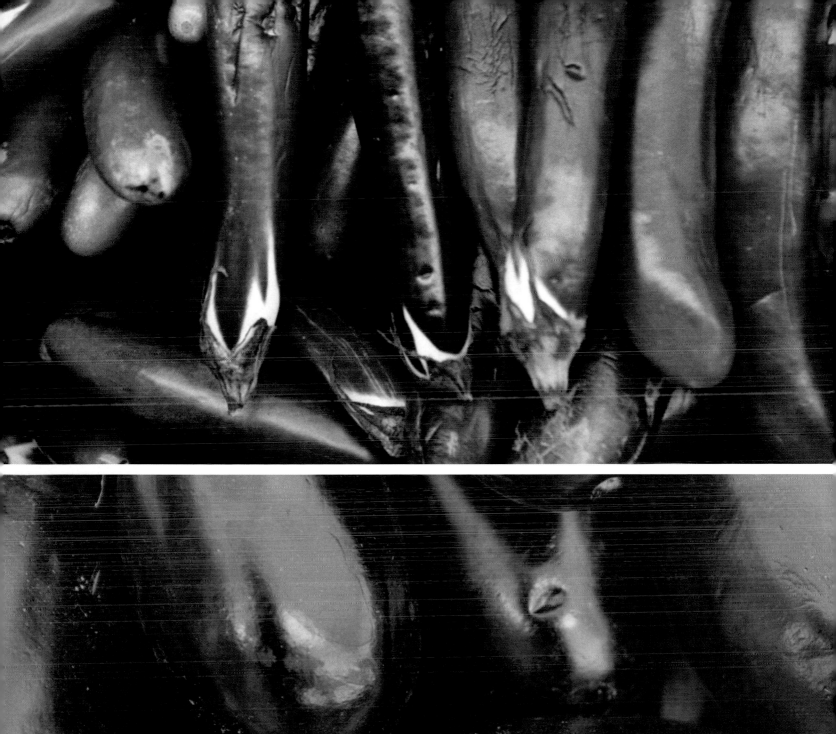

For a vegetable, eggplant has a lot of mystique.
(Boston Globe photos/ John Blanding, Pat Greenhouse)

SEPTEMBER

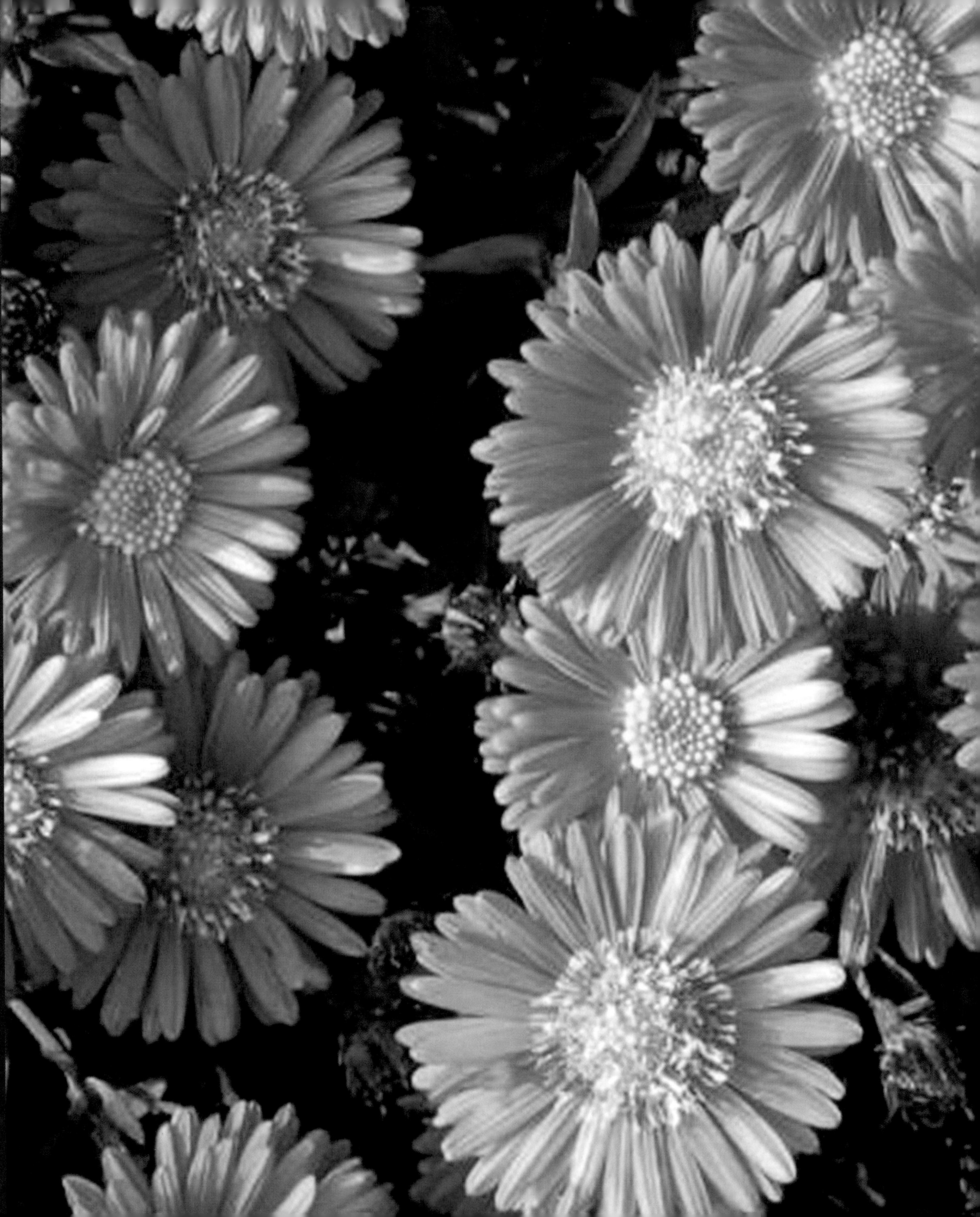

Introducing the Fall Lines

FALL IS A TIME WHEN EVERYTHING COMES TOGETHER in some gardens, with all the warm fall hues melding effortlessly under a clear, blue sky. It's also a time when some gardens fall apart. The difference is planning.

I remember the first year I gardened, sitting in my backyard one September day, staring grimly at a single yellow snapdragon, the only thing blooming. Without any plan, I'd simply bought all my favorite perennials. Unfortunately, they all bloomed in June.

After that, I went on a hunt for perennials that flower in autumn and found quite a few. Some, such as New England asters and helenium, are well known. Others remain under-appreciated, including the spectacular 4-foot blue autumn monkshood (Aconitum carmichaelii) and the most beautiful of all fall flowers, the white cupped Japanese anemone variety 'Honorine Jobert.'

Now is the time to assess your yard and take note of what you need to carry it successfully through fall, since September is one of the best months for planting perennials and shrubs.

**Left: Asters are a popular fall-flowering perennial.
(Photo courtesy of Proven Winners® – www.provenwinners.com)**

There have never been so many choices or styles for autumn gardens. They can still be as traditional as cushion mums and pumpkins. But they can also include tall borders of native perennials and ornamental grasses that flutter and buzz with bird and insect life. Today's options also include flamboyant tropical foliage plants that brazenly complement swimming-pool areas and modern architecture until the first frost. Textured dwarf evergreens are just beginning to become part of the scene, too.

During the last quarter-century, many good fall perennials have entered the nursery trade, notably boltonia, iron weed, maroon-leaved 'Hillside Black Beauty' Cimicifuga simplex (also called actaea), Joe Pye weed, 'Firetail' mountain fleece (Persicaria amplexicaulis) and 'Chocolate' Eupatorum rugosum. Many are native plants. Giant hibiscus is an old-fashioned mallow that has staged a comeback. Breeders are selecting and introducing other types of native asters besides the familiar New England aster. 'October Skies' and 'Raydon's Favorite' are two sky-blue selections of the wild Aster oblongifolius that are gaining popularity. So is 'Lady in Black,' an Aster lateriflorus selection with handsome maroon foliage and small, creamy flowers.

Chrysanthemums continue in popularity, "but you have to be selective. A lot of mums are ho-hum," says Paul Miskovsky of Miskovsky Landscaping in Falmouth, MA. He favors long-lived Chrysanthemum ponicum and Korean daisy mums such as 'Sheffield.'

Ornamental grasses, which are at their best in the fall,

Below: 'Purple Dome' is a shorter selection of our native New England Aster (Aster nova-angliae).
(Boston Globe photo/ Suzanne Kreiter)

swept into popularity in the 1980s and have remained fixtures among good and lazy gardeners alike. (Most are unkillable and as hard to remove as a tree stump.) They lend a casual meadow effect to many suburban gardens that might otherwise seem stiff. Foxtail ornamental grass (pennisetum), black-eyed Susans and maroon 'Autumn Joy' sedum have become a standard low-maintenance combination in thousands of home landscapes. Popular newer sedum varieties with purple foliage include 'Purple Emperor' and 'Matrona,' while 'Frosty Morn' has white flowers and variegation.

In the 1990s, annuals regained popularity. Most flag as fall days grow shorter, except for the new tropical annuals, which are mostly just perennials from warmer regions. These great fall performers don't know what winter is, so they grow and bloom vigorously until the first frost catches them by surprise and turns them to blackened mush. Before then, however, some reach impressive size. You now find very untraditional New England fall gardens that can be punctuated by 12-foot banana trees, jaunty red-leaved caster bean plants, and sinister brugmansia, whose huge fragrant trumpets wait in vain to be pollinated by tropical bats. September was never like this before.

The '90s also saw the explosion of container gardening and the reappearance of tropical (or "summer") bulbs such as dahlias and cannas that once made Victorians swoon. Modern gardeners who have learned to winter over brugmansias indoors are no longer intimidated by the idea of digging up and storing frost-sensitive dahlia tubers in the basement.

The emerging stars of contemporary fall gardens are shrubs, especially dwarf needled evergreens. Mainstream gardeners are just beginning to notice the plethora of interesting shapes, textures and colors of conifers developed by a longtime core of ardent specialists and collectors. Many are small enough to plant in the middle of a perennial border. If your autumn garden is always in danger of falling apart (if for no other reason than that fall perennials are tall and prone to toppling), nothing holds it all together better visually than a few well-placed solid evergreen specimens. And they give winter interest, too.

The Juniperus virginiana variety 'Gray Owl,' a fine-texture lacy-blue evergreen that grows a couple of feet tall and then spreads out, is a favorite of at least one gardening expert I know. So is the dwarf Colorado blue spruce, especially the Pica pungens variety 'Montgomery.'

Korean fir (Abies koreana) is an elegant, very slow-growing evergreen whose dark-violet cones look almost like flowers. It has won both the coveted Styer Award of the Pennsylvania Horticultural Society and the Cary Award started by the Worcester County Horticultural Society in

Massachusetts, whose committee particularly recommends the variety 'Horstman's Silberlocke,' which has dark green needles curled backward, exposing silver bands underneath.

Shrubs are the easiest plants to garden with, requiring less weeding and watering than perennials and a faster payoff than trees. But the problem with deciduous flowering shrubs is that most bloom in the spring. So wholesalers have searched out fall-blooming shrubs. The new blue hydrangea called 'Endless Summer' is supposed to bloom summer through fall.

But the champions for autumn bloom are such recent varieties of Pee Gee hydrangeas as pink-white 'Tardiva' and the even later chartreuse 'Limelight.' Seven son flower (hepticodium), chaste bush (vitex) and butterfly bush (Buddleia davidii) have all recently gained popularity because of their late flowers, as have the small "subshrubs" caryopteris and perovskia, which are pruned halfway back in early spring. Try fothergilla, Virginia sweetspire and oakleaf hydrangeas for their rich fall foliage. ❧

Watch for Invaders

OF ALL PEOPLE, GARDENERS KNOW BEST how quickly plants can get out of control.

We've all had plants that took advantage of our hesitant hospitality. There's that multiflora rosebush that sprouted unbidden and was such a hit with the mockingbirds that you let it stay, and now it's big and thorny enough to guard Sleeping Beauty's castle. Meanwhile, baby rose canes are reaching out to grab you from every unpatrolled niche, spread by those ungrateful mockingbirds.

So how do you tell an overly aggressive and invasive plant from a desirable one? This isn't an easy question. You don't have to graduate from West Point to be able to weed a garden, but you do need to be able to recognize the enemy.

Strangely enough, the most important war on weeds today is being waged not in our yards but on conservation land and along shorelines, where invasive species are taking over about 10 million acres nationally each year. The most visible example of this is the miles of purple loosestrife in bloom throughout many of our wetlands. Twenty years ago these were diverse habitats; then, almost overnight, they became solid purple.

"It's like 'The Invasion of the Body Snatchers,' " says Tim Simmons, a restoration ecologist with the Massachusetts Natural Heritage and Endangered Species Program. "Overnight you realize you have a problem. We don't know when a new plant that existed in sparse amounts will suddenly explode. They seem to reach a critical mass and go crazy."

In many woods today, walkers will find themselves tripping on honeysuckle and bittersweet vines busy smothering trees, or being stuck by increasingly impenetrable thickets of thorny multiflora roses, buckthorns and Japanese barberries. Bamboo-like Japanese knotweed has been around for 100 years, but in the last 10 it's spread to every major river system in Massachusetts. Like the worst invasives, it pushes out all other vegetation, rendering natural areas useless for most wildlife and recreation.

One irony is that many of these invaders originated in our own gardens, even though we usually think of our garden plants as fragile, cultivated creatures under relentless attack from wild weeds. The wild plants of forest and field are being overwhelmed by some of the most aggressive

Above: Invasive Japanese knotweed seldom spreads by seed but commonly relies on people who cut down live stalks and dump them where they can sprout new colonies. (Boston Globe photo/ Joanne Rathe)

Left: Japanese knotweed in bloom, with fleecy white flowers. (Boston Globe photo/ David Kamerman)

cultivated plants, especially those imported from other parts of the world that don't have insects and diseases here to keep them in check.

Nowhere is this truer than among homes close to conservation land and waterways. It's a status symbol today to clear a lot and build a house snug against protected land so you don't have to worry about other builders compromising your privacy and natural view. Most people don't consider that the plants landscaping these new homes pose a threat to those very natural areas.

OK, but won't nature just find a new balance? After all, most of our ancestors weren't native to these shores either. Isn't this just evolution?

These are actually profound questions, because what's happening to southern New England's wild areas is happening all over the world as global trade facilitates the spread of species. To put it simply, some ecologists think we may end up with the same plants, animals and bugs all over the world, as the toughest arrivals invade new areas and overwhelm the daintier local flora and fauna, similar to what has happened in Hawaii.

Of course, plants from India and Brazil aren't likely to take over an area like New England where the climate is so different. Most of the invasive life-forms we see in the Northeast are from similar temperate regions such as

Above: Birds spread the pretty orange berries of Oriental bittersweet, which is one of the worst invasives because it kills mature trees. (Photo courtesy of Massachusetts Audubon Society)

Northern Europe, China and Japan.

What's most undesirable about this scenario, of course, is mass extinctions. The world would become an even more homogenized place, with a few super-successful species circling the globe.

Not only would there be a Gap store at every mall, but Norway maples in every forest, which, locally speaking, would be a letdown for people who like the orange fall foliage of our retreating native sugar maples, not to mention maple syrup on their pancakes.

The most hopeful strategy is to import some natural enemies of invasives. This is called "biological control." But in the short term what can gardeners do to help protect wild areas in their neighborhoods? They can remove invasive plants from their properties so they aren't jumping-off points, says Simmons.

He advises homeowners to get rid of their multiflora rose, Norway maple, Oriental bittersweet, porcelain berry, Morrow's honeysuckle (as well as Tatarian, Amur and Japanese honeysuckles), burning bush (also known as winged euonymus), Japanese knotweed, autumn olive, black locust, black swallowwort, common and Japanese barberry (including those colored varieties), common and glossy buckthorn, garlic mustard, goutweed (also known as bishop's-weed), purple loosestrife and yellow water iris (Iris pseudocorus).

Other plants Simmons suggests gardeners avoid, as they may eventually become problems here, include kiwi vine, rugosa rose, Japanese and common hedge privet, Japanese hops, creeping buttercup, chervil (Anthriscus sylvestris), Lysimachia nummularia, silver lace vine, sycamore maple, tree of heaven, wild thyme, white mulberry and Western catalpa trees, and Myosotis scorpioides.

"I have some people telling me they can't even grow some of these plants, so how can they be a problem? It depends on where you live and the types of habitats around you. Flood plains, woodlands and wetlands are particularly vulnerable," says Simmons. "Also, individuals dumping yard wastes in natural areas are a real problem."

Invasives are super tough, so just occasional cutting back usually only encourages their roots to grow larger and the plants to become more vigorous. The root must be killed.

If a plant is too large to pull by hand, the best way to uproot medium-size shrubs and small trees is with a weed wrench, a large lever that almost effortlessly pops the entire root systems of honeysuckles, buckthorns and barberries out of the ground.

Invasives can come back to life after you think you've killed them, so don't toss them aside; they'll probably just reroot. And don't add them to usable compost piles.

Herbicides are the easiest way to kill roots, and any homeowner is free to apply herbicides on his or her property, provided they're handled responsibly. Glyphosate, which

Above: Once established, Japanese knotweed is almost impossible to eradicate. (Boston Globe photo/ Joanne Rathe)

breaks down into harmless molecules in 40 to 60 days, is the active ingredient in Monsanto's popular Roundup, the workhorse of herbicides, and Rodeo, which is safer to use around wetlands. Triclopyr is the active ingredient in Weed-Be-Gone and Brush-Be-Gone, which unlike glyphosate is effective on most woody plants except Oriental bittersweet.

When spraying herbicides, an expert recommends you wear hospital gloves inside elbow length pesticide gloves, eye protection, a dust mask, long pants and long-sleeved shirt to be washed separately from family laundry. Also carry an eye wash.

Among the better tools are "weed wands" that allow you to touch an herbicide-soaked sponge to herbaceous weeds such as chervil and garlic mustard while standing.

For large, problem trees such as buckthorn, tree of heaven, black locust and Norway maple, chop a few gashes into the trunks in late fall when sap is flowing back into the roots, then paint the wounds with herbicide. To cover extensive areas of woodland there are industrial strength tools such as "hypohatchets," which can chop gashes into the tree while injecting it with glyphosate, and the "EZject," which drives small pellets of herbicide into tree trunks.

Ridding even a modest backyard of potentially invasive plants can take years, warns Simmons. Though he spends his days patrolling state lands for invasives, he says, "I'm still in the process of eradicating all these plants from my own yard." ❀

'MOST UNWANTED' LIST

According to MassWildlife, some of the most difficult plants to kill include:

BARBERRY. These prickly plants must be pulled up by the roots. Use a weed wrench for fully grown shrubs.

BUCKTHORN. Cut stems and apply herbicide to the stumps in late fall.

GARLIC MUSTARD. This garlic-smelling biennial with four white petals out-competes native wildflowers in shady woodlands. Hand pull or apply herbicide to rosettes of basal leaves during late fall or early spring, and repeat for two to five years as new seeds sprout.

HONEYSUCKLES. Uproot shallow-rooted shrubs such as Lornicera morrowii, L. tatarica, L. maackii and L. xbella by hand or with a weed wrench.

JAPANESE KNOTWEED. A minimum of four cuttings annually for several years is required to deplete underground rhizomes. Occasional sporadic cutting back may be counterproductive. For faster results, pour herbicide into the hollow canes after cutting. Dispose of cut canes carefully in trash bags as they can start new colonies

MULTIFLORA ROSE. It blooms once a year with clusters of many white flowers, and produces tiny red hips. The stems look feathery at the base of each leaflet. Hand pull young plants. Use a machete, not a chain saw, to cut through thorny branches to get to the trunk in late fall, when it can be pulled with a weed wrench, or cut and paint the cut stem with herbicide.

ORIENTAL BITTERSWEET. This fast-growing vine can choke young trees and smother vegetation, interfering with the natural succession of forest regeneration. Because of its many underground runners, it often requires the application of glyphosate to freshly cut stems at the time of the first killing frost, usually in early October, to destroy established plants. Because the bright orange berries are viable, don't use them in holiday decorations.

PURPLE LOOSESTRIFE. Uproot when first seen because it's almost impossible to remove once established. Each plant produces up to 2 million seeds. Nursery hybrids are not necessarily sterile.

GARDENER'S WEEK 1

Design: Work on a landscape plan for fall planting of perennials, trees and shrubs.

Grapes: Leave them on the vine until they are almost bursting.

Lawn: It's time to overseed. Shop at garden centers that stock lawn seed mixes for New England, just make sure the package is dated this year and contains at least 50 percent combined fine fescues and bluegrasses, the best grass types for this region. They complement each other because the Kentucky bluegrass has the best all-around color and texture while the fescues are more tolerant of shade, drought and acid or infertile soil. Avoid mixes with more than 25 percent perennial ryegrass, or more than 1 percent weed or "crop" seeds (they list this). Use a shade mix if your lawn gets three to six hours of sun a day; any lawn getting less sun than that needs to be overseeded every year just to look so-so. Whether

you're patching, overseeding or starting a new lawn, the basic procedures are the same: A spreader will help seeds achieve even distribution. The key is to get the grass seed in contact with the soil. If you're patching bare spots, rake in the seed so it's slightly covered with soil, then firm it with the back of your rake. For seeding large areas, rent a slice-seeder – it looks like a mower with a seed hopper and plants your seeds at the proper depth. Make at least two passes, the second at a 45-degree angle to the first. Lightly mulching with hay will help prevent birds from eating the grass seed. Once planted, keep the seeds moist until they sprout. Fall rains should help with this.

Perennials: Keep the garden looking lush by cutting off any leaves and flower stalks of perennials that have turned brown or tattered. Cut back disfigured, aging foliage of columbine, delphinium,

hollyhock, malva and perennial geranium and they will produce fresh new leaves, and sometimes new flowers.

Tomatoes: Pinch off the tops of tomato plants and the new flower buds to hasten ripening of existing fruit.

Vegetables: Plant seeds of mache, spinach, arugula and radish. Pinch off the tips of Brussels sprout plants for larger sprouts and harvest them from the bottom up as they mature. Don't harvest winter squash or pumpkins until they attain their full mature coloring or after the first light frost.

Vegetable pests: The safest pesticide on vegetables is liquid dishwashing soap mixed with water and sprayed on sucking insects. Use this soap spray on spittle bugs, thrips, aphids and white flies. Use Bacillus thuringiensis (B.t.) where you see the holes of green or white

cabbage worm caterpillars in the leaves of broccoli, kale and cauliflower. Handpick tomato hornworms, cabbage worms and Colorado potato beetles.

Above photos, left to right:

Red fountain grass

Black-eyed Susans

Giant dahlias

Gourds

Chrysanthemums

Maple leaf

(Grass photo courtesy of www.parkseed.com; Boston Globe photos/ Matthew J. Lee, Joanne Rathe, Pam Berry, Wendy Maeda, Janet Knott)

GARDENER'S WEEK 2

Chrysanthemums: These really act more like disposable annuals than true perennials. Plant them in flower beds before the third week in September if you want to increase the slim odds they'll return next spring. They look taller if you just leave them in their pots instead of planting them in the ground. You can dot them around the garden or patio that way and just throw them in the compost pile after they finish blooming.

Houseplants: Take cuttings from coleus, annual geraniums and begonias to propagate favorite varieties. Young plants will usually fare better indoors over the winter than most mature ones.

Lawns: Most homeowners believe spring is the season for lawn care, but autumn is actually the better time for effective turf maintenance. Applications of fertilizer between now and November will help grass survive winter and green up more quickly in the spring. Look for lawn fertilizers that are organic or slow release. Another way to give your lawn a boost is to rent a core aerator in early September, which cuts plugs from the turf and deposits them on the surface, reducing compaction and invigorating grass roots.

Perennials: Deadhead echinacea and heliopsis to keep them blooming. Cut back summer perennials that have finished flowering so their tattered foliage does not detract from fall bloomers. This is a good time to plant mail-ordered Oriental poppies, large spring-blooming bleeding hearts and bearded iris.

TOP 10

Essential tools for growing backyard flowers or vegetables:

10 **Cultivators.** Many veterans have a soft spot for the traditional three- or four-pronged cultivator, which also aerates the soil as it loosens weeds.

9 **Hoes.** Whereas cultivators loosen the roots of large weeds so you can pull them up, hoes decapitate small weeds.

8 **Shovels.** For heavy work, such as digging a bed, you need a shovel, and preferably someone else to use it. Buy shovels, spades and spading forks with a strengthening metal shank that extends partway up the handle.

7 **Spades.** A spade differs from a shovel because its head is flat instead of curved. It's good for edging grass and for digging a hole you put a plant in.

6 **Spading forks.** People used to call these pitchforks. They're handy for lifting and dividing perennials without severing roots, for turning compost, and for breaking up soil.

5 **Rakes.** You want the plastic type for raking fallen leaves off the lawn, but for flower and vegetable gardening you need a metal flat-backed rake.

4 **Trowels.** These are essential for digging small holes for planting.

3 **Hoses.** Watering cans are picturesque, but nozzle, spray and sprinkler attachments make hoses more practical and versatile.

2 **Wheelbarrows.** A metal contractor's wheelbarrow will carry compost, plants and other tools down narrow garden paths, and is a useful container for mixing.

1 **Pruners.** There are different kinds, including loppers, shears and saws. But most essential are the hand clippers: Never walk through the garden without them.

GARDENER'S WEEK 3

Biennials: Finish planting young foxgloves, hollyhocks, cup-and-saucer campanula, wallflowers and other biennials that will bloom next year. Biennials generally need to be planted earlier in the fall than true perennials.

Deer: If they've been a problem for you, plant flowers this fall that aren't their favorites. For instance, select daffodils instead of tulips, allium instead of crocus, astilbe or bleeding heart instead of hosta. Salvias and asters also top a long list of plants that are resistant to deer, and the animals avoid most herbs with fragrant leaves.

Flower arranging: As ornamental grasses come into flower, try adding some of their inflorescence to informal country-style bouquets that might include black-eyed Susans and sunflowers. Sprays of flowering herbs such as purple oregano will add scent. Pair purple or bronze foliage from plants such as perilla or purple-leaved smoke bush with fiery-red or orange dahlias. Mix pastel flowers with the silver foliage of plants such as dusty miller and other types of artemisia.

Houseplants: Bring them indoors when nighttime temperatures stay around 45 degrees. But first prune them back and inspect them for pests and diseases. Spray all except succulent types with water mixed with insecticidal soap.

Lawn: Finish lawn restoration in the next two weeks. A dense lawn has fewer weeds. Target problem areas where turf is thin or brown or displaced by weeds. Most lawn weeds are annuals and will soon die. Nature abhors a vacuum, so plant grass seed in these soon-to-be vacated patches this weekend and there will be no room for crabgrass to sprout next spring. If you have a problem area due to heavy foot traffic, do what athletic field managers do and use a "sports turf" seed blend of rye and bluegrasses designed to withstand rough treatment. If your trouble spot suffers from too much shade, overseed (as noted in Week 1) with a grass mix especially formulated for shade, or just give up and replace the lawn with a shade-tolerant ground cover such as vinca or pachysandra.

Shrubs: Finish planting or moving evergreens by mid-October. But with deciduous shrubs it's better to wait until they lose their leaves before you transplant them.

Spring flowering bulbs: Plant the diminutive early-spring bloomers such as snowdrops, scilla and crocus in large drifts this month. You can site these under deciduous trees because they will bloom before the trees leaf out. Many digging rodents eat crocus corms, but one way to deter them is by placing obstacles in the planting hole such as thorny rose bush trimmings or gravel.

Above photos, left to right:

Gated vegetable garden

White-tailed deer

Eupatorium

Ruby Swiss chard and scarlet salvia

Verbena

Red cabbage

(Boston Globe photos/ Jonathan Wiggs, Mark Wilson, Suzanne Kreiter; verbena photo courtesy of Proven Winners® – www.provenwinners. com; red cabbage photo courtesy of www.park-seed.com)

GARDENER'S WEEK 4

Deer: If they're giving the evergreens in your tall hedge the appearance of green lollipops by stripping the bottom 6 feet of greenery, consider planting a row of evergreen pieris before mid-October or next spring at the base of the hedge to hide the naked limbs. These attractive, broad-leaved evergreens flower in April and are truly deer-proof. Water newly planted evergreens weekly until the ground freezes. Heaviest deer browsing begins in October and continues through the winter, so start spraying evergreens with a deer repellent now. You can also surround individual evergreens or hedges with a tight wrapping of nearly invisible deer fencing.

Herbs: Pot up garden-grown rosemary, chives and parsley to move indoors to a sunny windowsill. Snip leaves from other culinary herbs and keep them in the freezer for winter use.

Lawn: If you've already planted new grass seed, use a starter fertilizer for seedlings after they have sprouted. Otherwise, fertilize with a slow-release, high-nitrogen synthetic fertilizer or an organic fertilizer such as cottonseed meal, manure or Milorganite. Or use a "bridge mix" that combines a synthetic fertilizer for fast greening with low-acting organic fertilizer to help plants through the winter. Look for the words "slow release," "time release" or "encapsulated" on labels of chemical fertilizers so the nitrogen doesn't wash out and pollute watersheds.

Perennials: Lift and divide crowded clumps of spring- and summer-blooming perennials. This is also a great time to buy new perennials, which are often on sale and can be safely planted through October.

Weeds: This is a good time to go after stubborn perennial weeds such as chickweed, dandelion, dock, wild garlic, hawkweed, ground ivy, plantain, thistle and sorrel, which are especially vulnerable to root kill from spot applications of broadleaf herbicides now. But if you planted grass seed this fall, wait until spring to use herbicides. The two don't mix.

Window boxes: The traditional solution to seasonal change is still a good one: Dump the contents of your faltering window box display into your compost pile, and then fill the planter with pots of chrysanthemums or ornamental kale and cabbages. There are now mini-kales just the right size for window boxes.

Dahlias (Dahlia).

No flower offers more variety in size, shape and color. Dwarf bedding types bloom earliest, but I prefer taller varieties with decorative maroon foliage such as 'Bishop of Landaff.' You can treat these tropicals as annuals or dig up their tubers (roots) to store over the winter.

(Boston Globe photos/ Matthew J. Lee, Joanne Rathe)

OCTOBER

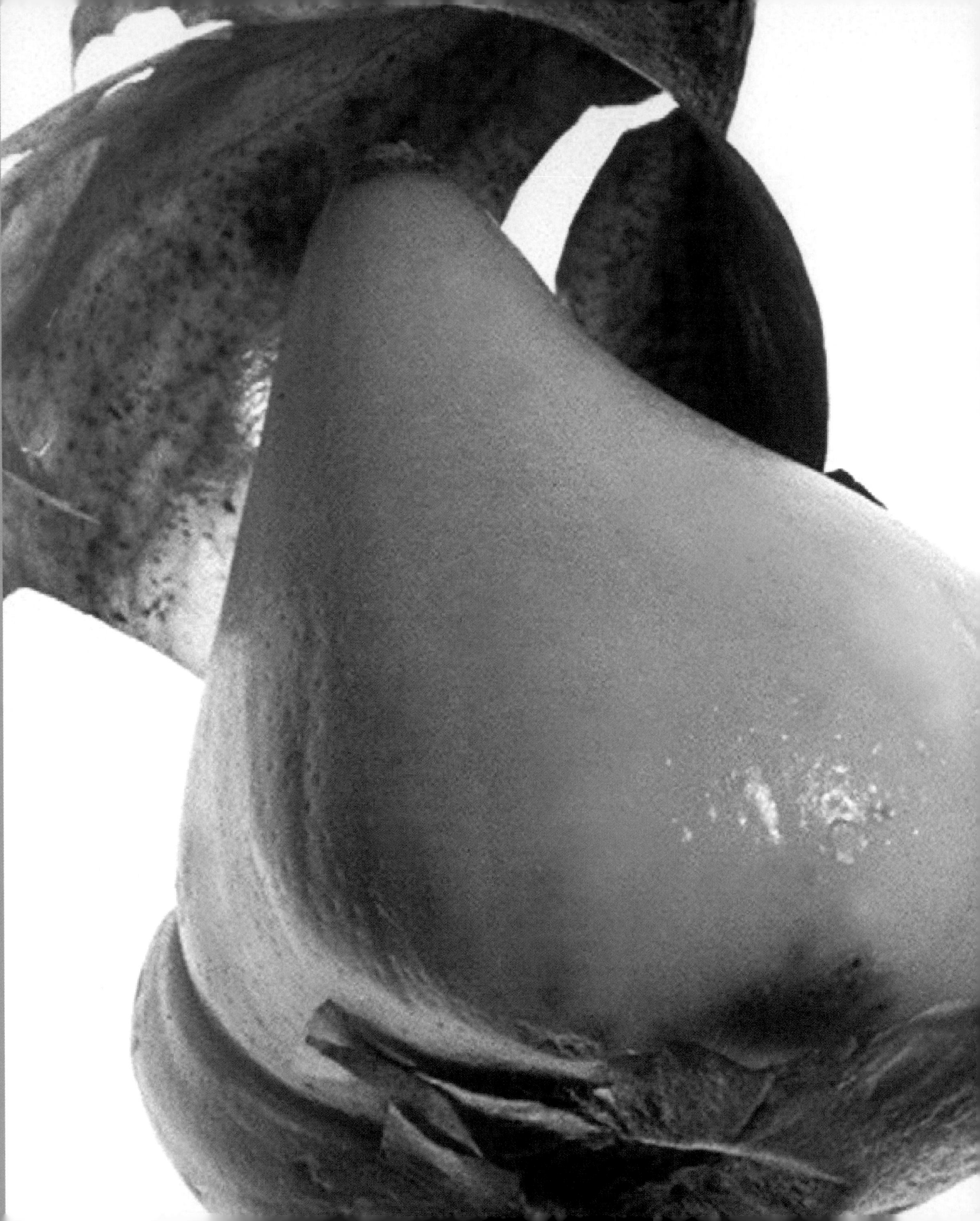

TIPTOE THROUGH TULIP SELECTION

MOST OF YOUR SPRING-BLOOMING BULBS SHOULD BE IN THE GROUND BY NOW. But you can still plant tulips through the middle of November to get a fine show next April and May.

But which varieties of tulips should you buy? Few flowers come in as many varieties of colors and shapes. It would take a lifetime to try them all.

One great thing about tulips is that they're almost foolproof. The bulbs arrive from Holland with their flowers for next year already packed embryonically inside, ready to perform next spring.

The problem usually comes the second and third spring after planting, when many tulips perform poorly, if at all. Eventually, all you'll get is a crop of leaves with no flower buds. Pull them out at that point, or else the foliage will continue to come up for years, raising your hopes and taking up garden space, but never flowering again.

Left: Tulip bulbs look easy enough, but they require advanced thinking to be truly foolproof. (Boston Globe photo/ John Blanding)

This is why experienced gardeners often chose tulip bulbs on the basis of staying power. For instance, 'Apricot Beauty' may be one of the most appealing tulips, its unique golden peach shade perfect with daffodils, but gardeners for whom it has failed to bloom a second year often shun it thereafter for better performers.

DEEP PLANTING

Twenty five years ago I was putting in a peony hedge and planted some tulips at the bottom of the 20-inch-deep trench I'd prepared, before backfilling with rich soil and shallowly planting the peonies. I used several kinds of then-new Darwin hybrid tulips that were being toted as taller, larger, earlier and in most ways more wonderful than older tulip varieties. Responding to the ecstatic catalog prose, I ordered 'Big Chief,' described as rosy-salmon pink; 'Parade,' a brilliant red; 'Daydream,' described as a deep pastel apricot; and 'Orange Sun.'

What I got the following spring were four almost indistinguishable shades of brilliant orange-red. That's when I learned to take catalog descriptions with a grain of salt. Darwin hybrids are great, but a wide variety of colors they have not.

The good news is that the 'Parade' Darwin hybrids that had been planted in the sunniest spot came up for 20 years with those big orange-red blooms. They remind me of the Ford pickup my husband got 250,000 miles on.

I had heard that deep planting prolongs the life of tulips, and based on my experience, that seems to be true. Nevertheless, no one in their right mind is going to dig a 20-inch hole just to plant tulips.

But it's no harder to plant long-lived types like Darwin hybrids at the usual 8-inch depth than to buy short-term performers.

There are many individual varieties of tulips that have bloomed four years or more in trials. True, most of them tend toward orange, but if you're one of the many who prefer pastel tulips, there are a few of them on the list of long-term performers, too.

Other things you can do to maximize your investment include paying less for your bulbs. It's not too late to order through the mail from some of the wholesale dealers who vend bulbs for half what they cost in garden centers, and have many more varieties to choose from.

Select bulbs that are firm, heavy and unblemished, but don't worry if the brown papery outer sheaths are tattered or missing. If the ground has frozen hard, discard leftover bulbs or plant them in containers and put them outside. They will not survive the winter unplanted.

(Boston Globe photos/ John Blanding)

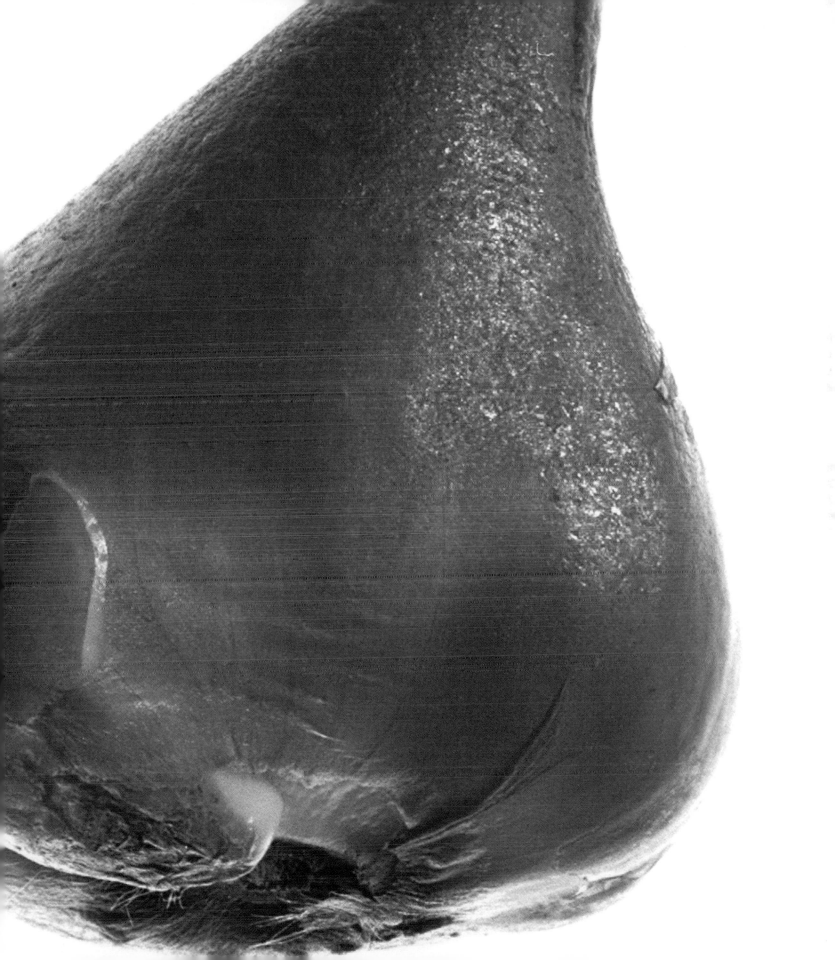

THE BEST RETURN VISITORS

All tulips will rot over the winter if planted in a poorly drained site such as a depression, and most require lots of sun. Given good conditions, here are some of the longest-lived varieties of tulips, according to tests in the United States and the Netherlands:

Botanical tulips are much smaller than hybrid tulips but also more truly perennial. The best include starry yellow and white 'Tarda,' tiny cream 'Turkestanica' and fragrant yellow 'Sylvestris.' These tulips bloom at various times in April and May.

Eight-inch-tall kaufmanniana tulips are among the first to bloom in early April with small waterlily-like flowers. 'Stresa' is yellow with a wide red central stripe on each petal. 'Heart's Delight' is carmine red and soft rose.

Single early tulips bloom more than two weeks in April and return well. Best performers include the antique varieties orange and purple 'Princess Irene,' fragrant orange 'General de Wet,' red and gold 'Keizerskroon' (circa 1750) and crimson 'Couleur Cardinal.'

Double early tulips also bloom in mid-April and last even longer. Golden yellow 'Monte Carlo' is the best repeater in this group.

April blooming Darwin hybrids are early, large and among the best repeaters. The orange and red shades are particularly good performers.

Triumph tulips bloom at the same time as Darwin hybrids, towards the end of April. They're not as large or as perennial, but they come in cool shades and pastels not available in Darwin hybrids. The best repeaters in this category include rose pink 'Don Quichotte,' pink-edged orange 'Jimmy,' white-edged lavender 'Dreaming Maid,' deep purple 'Negrita,' white-edged red 'Merry Widow' and red-edged yellow 'Thule.'

May-blooming Darwin tulips are later and smaller than Darwin hybrids. They come in a much greater range of colors but are generally not long lasting or good repeaters. Some exceptions are red 'Balalaika,' white 'Maureen,' red-edged white 'Merry Widow,' pink 'Rosy Wings,' red-flamed white 'Sorbet' and carmine red 'Renown.'

Double peony tulips are short, late bloomers with many petals. Fragrant pink 'Angelique' is the favorite in this category and also the best performer.

Lily-flowering tulips are among the last to bloom in late May. They're tall, long-lasting and good for cutting, with graceful pointed petals. The best repeaters include 'Red Shine,' 'White Triumphator,' white-edged violet 'Maytime,' white-edged magenta 'Ballade' and yellow 'West Point.'

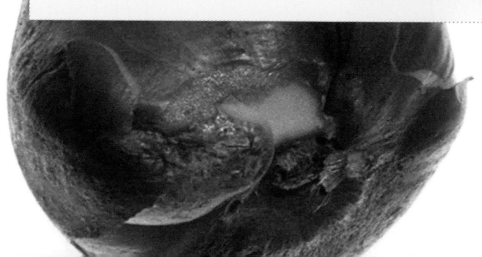

DIG IN

HOW TO PLANT BULBS:

Choose a well-drained site with at least four hours of sun. Don't plant bulbs where water collects or they'll rot.

Dig a hole that's three times as deep as the width of your largest bulbs. It's more efficient to use a long-handled shovel than one of the specialized bulb-planting tools on the market.

Mix about a quarter cup of bulb fertilizer or super phosphate and two cups of dampened peat moss into the 2 inches of soil at the bottom of the hole to provide nutrients and improve drainage. Mix in lime if your soil is acidic. Follow package directions for amounts.

Push the bottom of the bulbs into the loosened soil at the bottom of the hole. The pointed ends of the bulbs should face upward. Moisten the bottom of the hole slightly.

Mix dampened peat moss into the soil you've dug out and then refill the hole with it, burying the bulbs. The planted area should rise an inch above garden level to facilitate draining water.

Soak the mound of top soil thoroughly so the bulbs will settle in and start growing roots.

DEALING WITH PESTS:

Lilies get wiped out by the red lily leaf beetle and shouldn't be purchased unless you're willing to spray or hand pick these pests all season long. Lily leaf beetles will also feed lightly on fritillaria, Solomon seal and erythronium.

Deer will sample most plants but are tantalized by tulips. If you live in deer country, you may find you can't grow tulips unless you spray the leaves and flowers regularly with deer repellent.

Rodents do most of their damage feasting on bulbs underground. Soaking bulbs in a commercial deterrent such as Deter or Ropel before planting them will help. Planting large tulip bulbs (not species like tarda) extra deep – as in up to 18 inches – will help protect them from burrowers and also make them bloom for more years.

The only completely marauder-proof bulbs are the poisonous ones: snowdrops, daffodils, leucojum and fall-blooming crocuses (colchicums and sternbergias). However, there are many pest-resistant bulbs that wildlife find unappetizing. Try squills, alliums and chinodoxias if you have an animal problem.

EARLY BLOOMERS

Another trick is to plant early-flowering tulips rather than later types because the flowers last longer in cool weather. A mid-May heat wave can polish off late bloomers in a matter of days.

When you get your bulbs (and if time is running out go ahead and buy them at the local garden center), you're supposed to plant them 8 inches deep and 6 inches apart in a sunny site with good drainage, pointy ends up. The best locations are against the south side of a house or wall, where the reflected heat will help them bloom earlier, or on a hillside, which insures good drainage. I like to plant them where I can view them from the house.

When planting tulips in my perennial garden, I place them toward the rear. To induce tulips to bloom in future years you must let their foliage continue to photosynthesize until it turns yellow and brown. That takes a couple of months, during which the stalks and leaves get quite ugly, so you'll want them in the back where other foliage can grow up to hide them, not in the front row.

Some people treat tulips as annuals, planting them the quick and dirty way, 3 inches apart and 4 inches deep, knowing they'll still bloom fine their first spring. As soon as the flowers are through, these gardeners yank them out and send them to the compost pile. The pluses for doing this are easy planting, top-sized flowers and no ugly ripening foliage to look at through early summer. The big negative is the expense.

Except for wild botanical tulips, most varieties don't look right in a naturalized situation the way daffodils do. Tulips are much more formal-looking than daffodils.

For the best aesthetic results, plant tulips in groups of one color. It takes know-how or very specific color combinations to mix different tulips. Good combinations include 'White Triumphator' with pink 'Ballade' or 'Red Shine' lily-flowered tulips. White 'Mount Tacoma' with pink 'Angelique' double peony-flowered tulips is another winning combo. And actually, most Darwin hybrids do go well together. It's all that orange and red.

You can plant tulips in clusters or in formal rows, just make sure your rows are at least three deep and the tulips are staggered. Never plant tulips singly. The only thing that looks dumber than a lone tulip is a single row of tulips. Don't ask how I know.

The biggest work to planting tulips, of course, is to dig the holes.

Though I haven't been able to bring myself to treat tulips as annuals, I do now go to lengths to avoid digging holes just for them. Instead, I try to combine this activity with another goal, such as planting a peony hedge or dividing and resetting daylilies, or even planting shrubs or preparing next year's vegetable garden.

APPETIZERS

Personally, I don't think tulips are worth digging for. I think of them as irresistible but short-term and inexpensive, the nifty appetizer before the garden's main course arrives. I don't get dressed up and drive downtown to order an appetizer, but I never pass up the appetizer either – so I wouldn't miss an opportunity to stick a few tulip bulbs into any holes I'm digging in the fall. With all the planting and dividing that happens in autumn, my yard manages to absorb a few hundred tulip bulbs with surprising ease.

Even if I want to do a precise design with tulips, I try to get double or triple duty from my digging. Planting four quadrants of tulips (cherry red 'Kingsblood,' white 'Maureen,' apricot rose 'Menton' and carmine red 'Renown') in my front yard a number of years ago, I layered the 8-inch-deep trench with tulips on the bottom, then backfilled 5 inches and planted crocuses 3 inches down, backfilled some more, and then planted the surface with lamium 'White Nancy,' a well-behaved ground cover. I call this my layer-cake approach. And since any digging gives me the chance to enrich the soil with crumbly brown compost, I definitely end up with a chocolate layer cake.

Local voles and chipmunks have taken a toll on the crocuses since then, but the tulip bulbs seem too deeply planted to be bothered.

With big bold flowers on tall stalks so long before anything comparable blooms in the garden, tulips' temporary ways are worth putting up with. That is unless you are plagued with deer, who love to nibble off the buds just before the bloom. They, too, see tulips as great appetizers. ❁

Above: Cheery tulips in Boston's Copley Square result from October bulb planting. After blooming, the bulbs are replaced with summer annuals. (Boston Globe photo/ David L. Ryan)

Left: Tulips bloom through the snow. (Boston Globe photo/ Joanne Rathe)

LANDSCAPING FOR CURB APPEAL

WHEN IT COMES TO LANDSCAPING, most true gardeners think concerns about resale value are beside the point, like asking a fly fisherman how much he can get per pound for his trout.

Ideally, gardens should never be sold. They should be inherited and passed down, or endowed and open to the public. Or they should die with the gardener, who never gets sent away to a nursing home, but instead gets to enjoy her leafy paradise until the last mortal minute.

Of course, in modern suburbia, it's usually not that way. Homes are investment commodities that do double duty as family shelters. Even people who are deeply attached to their homes might think about cashing out and retiring to the Bahamas on the profit. Before then, most have a little bit of landscape tweaking to do.

It doesn't have to cost much to make a yard more inviting to buyers. In fact, it shouldn't. Homeowners who spent a few hundred dollars prepping their front and back yards for buyers increased their sales prices by more than double that amount, according to statistics from HomeGain national real estate consultants. The houses also sold faster.

If your concern is resale value, realtors say, focus on perfecting the "curb appeal" of the front yard: Tidy things up, have a great lawn, don't do anything idiosyncratic or out of keeping with your neighborhood, and don't spend too much.

"Landscaping has more value in a higher-end property than a lower-end property, say over $500,000," says Deirdre White, a real estate broker and appraiser. "But a lawn that's been taken care of is always one of the top 10 home improvements that boost your yield with minimal investment."

The perfect front lawn is so crucial to making a positive first impression on buyers, and so useless for anything else, that one wonders if it was invented purely for the purpose of selling real estate. In any case, don't buck the trend. Hire a lawn company to seed, fertilize and mow frequently until the sale is completed. An automatic sprinkler system is expected these days for high-end houses and will pay back its cost.

Don't confuse this kind of landscaping with gardening. Landscaping is something you hire professionals to do

Below: Spring and summer may be when it looks the best, but your yard should enhance your house all year round.

to make your land more attractive, usable and saleable. Gardening, on the other hand, is a do-it-yourself personal passion that seldom yields financial dividends. Few buyers will reward you for your devotion to your vegetable patch, your good taste in hostas or your Zen approach toward Japanese moss gardening.

If you're a plant collector, put it in the sale agreement that you're taking your favorites with you.

The exception is trees. Everyone likes them, they require little upkeep, and they're hard to kill. The most valuable kind you can own, in appraisal terms, is a beech.

"You can tie up $50,000 to $70,000 for one mature cutleaf, purple leaf or weeping beech," reports tree broker Rick Henkel of Princeton Horticultural Services in New Jersey, who locates large sought-after trees for landscape architects up and down the coast. "High-end residential people are looking for more and more substantial-sized trees so they don't have to wait for them to grow."

> **Most buyers like to see a nice flowering specimen tree.**

Most buyers like to see a nice flowering specimen tree on the front lawn and a grove of mature trees at the rear of the property creating a woodsy privacy screen, say realtors. Although a beech will take a lifetime to mature, Henkel says there are some trees that take hold quite rapidly and will be effective in two to five years, such as sugar maples, swamp maples ('Red Sunset' or 'October Glory') and lindens.

For fast-growing flowering specimen trees, Henkel recommends ornamental pears, though people have turned away from the 'Bradford' pear because of bad experiences with storm damage.

"The cultivars 'Cleveland Select' and 'Aristocrat' are much better," he says. "They grow fast, have spring flowers, and fall foliage. So do cornus kousa, halesia and oxydendrum. Crab apples lost popularity because they got diseases, but there are now excellent disease-resistant ones such as 'Donald Wyman.' Cherry trees are very popular. And magnolias oh, gosh - you can't find large ones, they're in such demand."

If you don't have much time and you need fast screening or tall vertical accents in a sunny spot, try ornamental grasses such as miscanthus. They mature in one season.

Most of the big bucks in landscaping, though, are spent on "hardscaping" rather than plants. Walkways and driveways, terraces and walls, pergolas and garden houses, pools and patios are all considered hardscaping. The more expensive the house, the more of these features it is expected to have.

Buyers with young children usually prefer space devoted to recreation rather than garden features if the property is small, says realtor Carol Brenner. She suggests vertical landscape accents: "Decorative fencing for privacy and aesthetic purposes always pays dividends no matter what size lot you have. Decks are always beautiful and you can decorate them with large pots of plants without sacrificing recreational area."

Kelleher believes gardens, like kitchens, are important but reach a point of diminishing returns if too much money is spent on them.

"You'll get the same money back if you spend $40,000 on a kitchen or $100,000," she says. "I am a gardener and I encourage all my owners to add wonderful landscaping. But when you put a lot of money into landscaping, you do not necessarily get it back. ... I've never had anyone say to me, 'I'm more concerned about the garden than the house.' The house always comes first." ❄

SPRUCING UP FOR A SALE

Here are some quick, inexpensive fixes for the landscape headed to market:

TIDY UP. Keep lawns immaculate, shrubs pruned, flower beds weeded and groomed. Replenish bark mulch and make sure any landscaping plastic is completely hidden from view. Remove eyesores such as dead tree limbs.

LIGHT THE OUTDOORS. Though open houses take place during the day, many serious buyers cruise by at night to check out neighborhood ambience. In addition to increasing security, do-it-yourself outdoor lighting kits can create evening landscape effects inexpensively. Placing a spotlight underneath a front yard tree so it shines up through the branches is especially effective in winter. Buyers like front lampposts, too. But don't use tacky-looking lights along the front walk or illuminate your yard like Fenway Park. Take your cue from surrounding front yards.

ACCENT WITH COLOR. Place clusters of large, attractive outdoor pots of seasonal flowers around the entryway and at other strategic spots on decks and patios. Many nurseries will plant pots for you. Or buy pots of tulips in the spring, annuals in the summer and mums in the fall. Keep them watered and replace them immediately when they're past their prime. Right now is a great time to add harvest accents such as pumpkins to your front yard. In winter, decorate the front of the house with an attractive door wreath and window boxes filled with cut evergreens and berries.

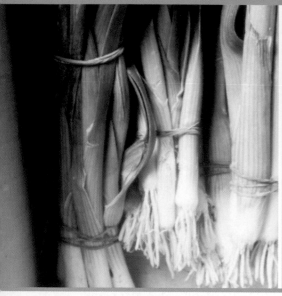

Gardener's Week 1

Composting: What about putting weeds in the compost bin? Actually, weeds with deep tap roots, such as dock, are loaded with minerals from the subsoil and make very beneficial compost. Most weeds are not a problem, particularly if they're pulled and added to the pile before they've gone to seed. There are some invasive ones you wouldn't want to compost; these include most vines and other plants that can sprout from a small piece of root such as poison ivy, bindweed, bittersweet, English ivy, ground ivy, goutweed or witch grass. Carefully dispose of the cut stalks of Japanese knotweed, which can produce new plants. If you have weeds with seeds, "cook" them in a tightly sealed black plastic bag in a sunny place until they turn to black goo before adding them to the compost bin. "Hot" composting, where the microbes are cranking so hard that they heat up the pile to 130 degrees or more, also kills most weed seeds and plant disease pathogens. Hot composting produces finished compost in only a few weeks, but it's a lot of work because you have to flip the pile with a hay fork every few days, so the material on the bottom ends up on top. It's good exercise and provides the aeration that makes microbes thrive, but most people just let the stuff sit and have a slower "cold" pile.

Lawn: Keep mowing as long as your grass continues to grow, but lower the height of the blade to 1 1/2 inches to make fall leaf raking easier. Run the gas tank empty before the mower is stored away for the year.

Vegetables: Harvest cabbage when the heads are softball size. No rush, as they can stand considerable frost. Harvest cauliflower when the buds are still tight, cutting off the entire head.

Water gardens: Take in tropical fish and tender aquatic plants from ornamental ponds. The fish can be stored in a tank using water taken from the pond. You can leave them outdoors for the winter if your water feature is 18 inches deep in places.

Woody plants: For the best tree and shrub varieties, look for tags indicating plants that are winners of the Pennsylvania Horticultural Society's Styer Gold Medals (www. pennsylvaniahorticulturalsociety. org/garden) and the regional Cary Award (www.caryaward. org) in Massachusetts. Both prizes are given to valuable but underused woody plants, but the Cary Award winners can generally tolerate colder temperatures.

Above photos, left to right:

Scallions

Aconitum uncinatum 'Wild Monkshood'

Fall vegetable harvest

Leaves for compost

Ornamental grass

(Boston Globe photos/ John Blanding, Jonathan Wiggs, Pam Berry; 'Wild Monkshood' photo courtesy of New England Wildflower Society/ William Cullina)

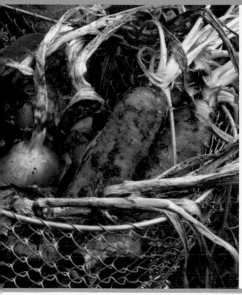

GARDENER'S WEEK 2

Annuals: Pull up and compost spent annuals. Harvest edible sunflower seeds.

Bulbs: Plant spring bulbs.

Cleanup: Start removing fallen leaves and garden debris that could harbor disease or insect pests.

Containers: For low-maintenance, year-round appeal, buy a pair of very large frost-proof plastic containers and plant them with dwarf Alberta spruce or blue holly in a soil-less potting mix to bracket your front door. Make sure the containers have drainage holes and keep them well watered.

Flowering cold-hardy vines for shade: If you don't have enough sun for climbing roses, consider the Japanese hydrangea vine (Schizophragma hydrangeoides). It wants to be 10 feet tall but you can prune it to 6 by 6 feet, and it doesn't even need a trellis to climb a wall. 'Moonlight' is the best cultivar; it has white fragrant flowers in July. Unfortunately, it can take seven years to bloom, but it also has pretty variegated foliage in the meantime. You need a trellis to try Dutchman's pipevine (Aristolochia macrophylla), which is also shade tolerant.

Lawn: Anytime is good to spread lime to reduce the acidity of lawns and gardens, which can be affected by acid rain. Lime also supplies calcium and magnesium. Dolomite lime is most commonly sold, but look for calcite lime as well, and use it every other time you apply lime. The ideal pH for lawns is 6.5-6.7, allowing grasses to make full use of the fertilizer. Because of acid rain, our soil grows more acidic with time, and tends to require 50 pounds of lime per thousand square feet of lawn every two to four years. But the only way to be sure what your lawn needs is to have your soil tested.

Mail-order detective work: How can you find unusual plants? Just Google their names to see which mail-order nurseries carry them. The Internet has transformed gardening along with everything else; now you can find and buy almost any plant that's offered by mail order, no matter how obscure.

Root pruning: Sever half the roots in a circle 2 feet from the trunk of small trees or shrubs you wish to move next year.

Roses: Prune rambler roses and any diseased or dead rose canes. October and November is the best time to plant "bare root" (mail order) roses.

Seeds: Collect seeds from annuals and perennials that you want to grow next year.

Tomatoes: Pick those showing color and let them finish ripening indoors, but not on a window sill or in direct sun.

Tools: For cleanup, use hoes or rakes that have long handles to avoid bending or stooping.

KNOW YOUR TERMS

DECIDUOUS: Trees and shrubs that lose their leaves in the winter.

EVERGREEN: Plants that retain some or all of their leaves in the winter.

GARDENER'S WEEK 3

Fall flowers: Evaluate what performed well for you over the long haul and plant more of these next year. Sweet alyssum, gaillardia, roses, ornamental grasses, autumn monkshood, sweet autumn clematis, perovskia, 'Autumn Joy' sedum, annual and perennial lobelia, Pee Gee hydrangea and `Stella d'Oro' daylily are all late-blooming troupers. Extra points go to spring-flowering perennials such as amsonia and geraniums that have colored fall foliage now. Visit other gardens and note what flowers are still in bloom this late in the season. You might want to try these next year.

Garlic: Plant before mid-November by separating large, healthy cloves from a garlic bulb and planting them pointy end up, 2 inches deep and 5 inches apart, in rich soil. Heads you buy in most supermarkets usually have been treated with growth inhibitors and are not hardy. Buy cold-hardy "hard neck"

(as opposed to "soft neck") varieties of garlic heads from a seed house, or from an organic/farmer's market.

Leaves: The best way to get rid of falling leaves is to turn them into micronutrient-rich soil for your lawn and garden. Just rake the leaves into a 3-foot-tall pile in an out-of-the-way spot and let nature takes its course. They'll break down into a 1-foot pile of leaf compost, called "leaf mold." (Don't pile them up against a building or a tree, which could rot.) Your compost will be ready in about 15 months if that's all you do. To speed the process, you can mow the leaves first, then add a shovel of good soil to the pile to introduce soil organisms. Watering the pile with a hose during summer dry periods will also speed composting. You don't need to buy a compost bin to make compost unless you're also composting fruit and vegetable scraps from the kitchen, in which case you should get a rodent-resistant bin with a cover.

New beds: Make new vegetable gardens and flower beds now, when the ground is relatively dry and easily worked, instead of in the spring when the soil will be soggier. Fall is also the most comfortable time to do heavy labor in the garden. Cut new beds out of the lawn with a square-end spade. Lift the top 3 inches of sod, shake loose soil back into the bed, and compost the grass and grass roots.

Shrubs: Plant or move shrubs or trees after they have lost their leaves. Wait until next spring, if possible, to plant evergreens.

Vegetables: Keep harvesting tomatoes as well as potatoes, radishes and rutabagas. Plant shallots and rhubarb. Encourage green tomatoes with a tinge of red to ripen by picking and wrapping them in paper, then placing them in drawers (not sunlight). Dig potatoes.

Above photos:

It's time for pumpkins, pumpkins and more pumpkins. Catch them transported in a tractor loader, grown big for bragging rights, and carved or painted up to serve as Jack-o'-lanterns.

(Boston Globe photos/ John Tlumacki, Wendy Maeda, Tom Landers, Tom Herde)

GARDENER'S WEEK 4

Cleanup: Cutting back the garden can be done in stages, removing the uglies first and leaving for later the plants that still have presentable seed heads and foliage. Ornamental grass, perennial geranium, artemisia and sedum are among the plants that keep looking great late into autumn. But eventually you'll want to cut it all down because it begins to look like debris. If you choose to wait until spring to do this, the dead leaves will act as mulch over the winter to insulate the roots from early thaws and frost heaves. It will also give birds a better opportunity to forage for seeds from last summer's flowers and to find shelter from predators and inclement weather at the same time. In either case, remove the top growth of disease-prone plants such as peonies, bearded irises, hollyhocks and phlox.

Jack-o'-lanterns: The trick to those intricate designs is to use a template. Select your design before you buy your pumpkin so the size and shape is right, or use a copying machine to change the template to the desired size. Glue your pattern onto the pumpkin with spray adhesive (which will wash off with the template after carving), then etch the design into the pumpkin's surface without cutting all the way through. The outlines will show up when you put a light inside. If you want a larger carving surface for a big design, cut the opening in the back of the pumpkin instead of the top and insert the light from the rear. Scoop out seeds. Apply petroleum jelly to cut surfaces to help seal in moisture for a longer-lasting Jack-o'-lantern.

Leaves: Whole leaves raked onto a garden can smother plants, but when leaves are shredded by a leaf vacuum or a lawnmower with a bag attachment first, you produce a superior alternative to expensive bark mulch for the garden and shrub border.

Low-maintenance gardening: List the plants that were easy and rewarding and those that were not worth the effort. Multiply the winners and eliminate the losers. Identify problem maintenance areas and consider adding paving or edging.

Multiflora rose: This prickly stemmed wild Asian rose is a dangerously invasive plant that grows to 9 feet tall and wide. It has numerous briefly blooming small white flowers in June, followed by reddish rose hips. Feathery fringes at the base of leaf stems distinguish it from all other roses. Long, arching stems and runners scramble over other plants to quickly create impenetrable thorny thickets. Seeds spread by birds soon sprout everywhere. Cut it down close to the ground between now and late October and paint the stump cut with Roundup. Or uproot it anytime with a wood wrench, a metal levering device also effective for pulling out other invasive shrubs such as burning bush, broom, Russian olive, Tartarian honeysuckle, barberry and buckthorn (www.weedwrench.com; 877-484-4177).

Tender bulbs: Lift tender summer bulbs such as gladiola, dahlia and canna with a garden fork after they've been blackened by frost. Cut off the tops, label them and let them dry in the sun. Don't shake off all the soil. After they've dried, store gladioli in open trays or hanging panty hose. Store dahlias in a box of very slightly damp peat moss.

PLANT OF THE MONTH

Goldenrod (Solidago).

A beautiful native flower, prized in foreign gardens but spurned at home because of the myth that it causes hay fever. Rich in nectar and high-protein pollen, it serves bees, butterflies and other insects with their last good meal before winter.

(Boston Globe photo/ John Tlumacki)

NOVEMBER

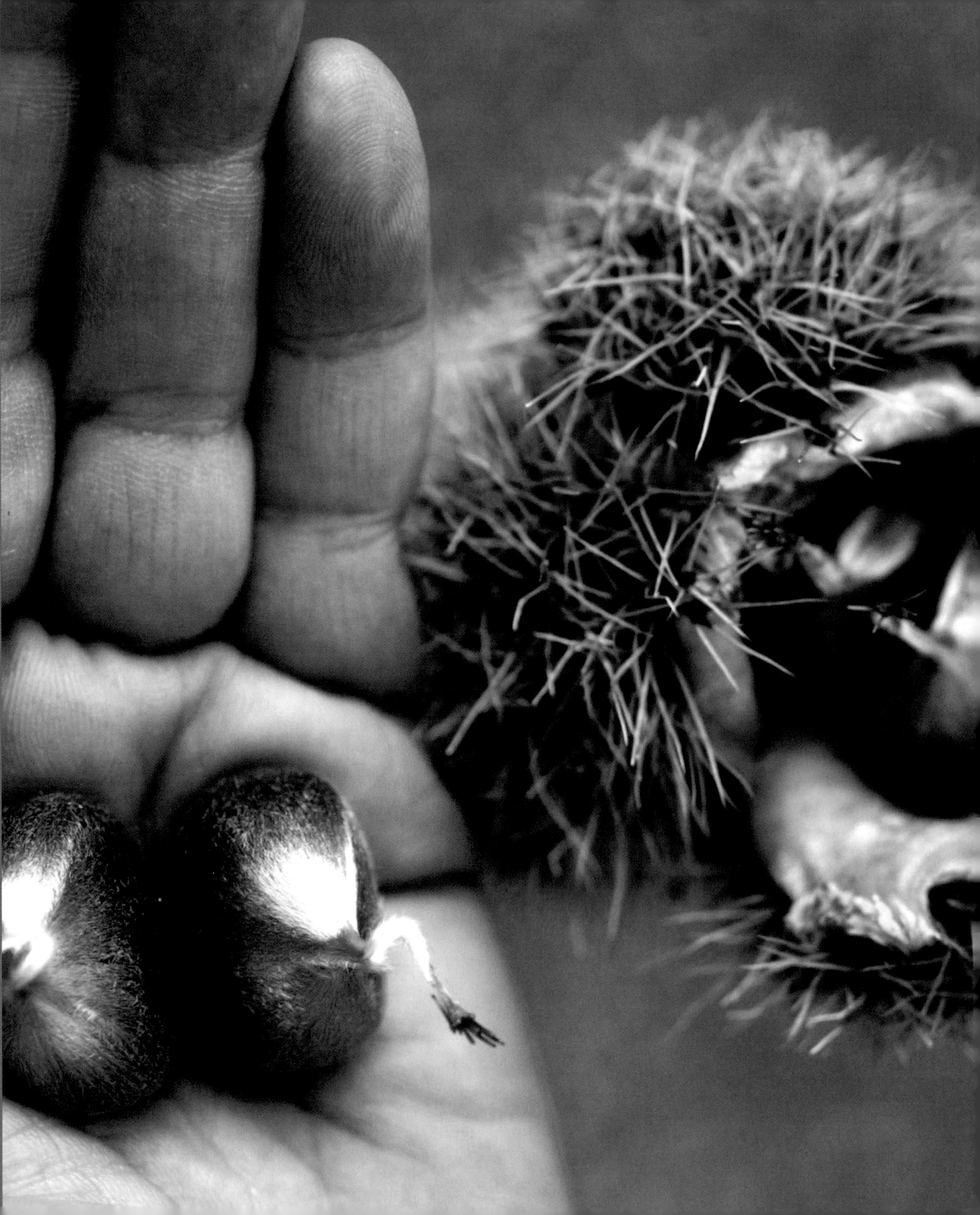

CAN THIS CHESTNUT BE SAVED?

CHESTNUTS ARE ASSOCIATED WITH THE HOLIDAYS, but the "chestnuts roasting on an open fire" in the old song are not the Chinese and Italian ones you buy in stores these days.

Very few people still alive have eaten a real American chestnut, the kind our great-grandmothers used in their Thanksgiving turkey stuffing. A blight arrived on imported Chinese chestnut trees in 1904 that wiped out our native trees, which had no resistance.

American chestnuts were once the single most important food source for native wildlife, as well as one of the most important crops for people. The tastiest of the world's chestnut varieties, they were our signature holiday food, roasted, boiled or ground into chestnut flour. Hundreds of millions of bushels were exported to Europe as a delicacy. One in four hardwood trees in America's eastern forest was a chestnut. Growing 100 feet tall and living to 400 years, they were called "the redwoods of the East," and it was said that a squirrel could travel from Maine to Georgia on the branches of chestnut trees without touching the ground. Their demise is still considered the most important species extinction in modern American history.

Left: A chestnut in the hand appears rounded after pollination. (Boston Globe photo/ Tom Landers)

But the story may yet have a happy ending. The American Chestnut Foundation is hybridizing trees that have all the characteristics of the American chestnut, but also the blight-tolerant genes from the Chinese chestnut.

"The American chestnut dating service" is what the Massachusetts Chapter calls its treasure hunt to find wild local chestnut trees of blooming age. If you think you've found one, consult www.masschestnut.org to report it. Just don't bother them with common horse chestnuts – those European trees with inedible nuts (called buckeyes, especially in Ohio) and spade-shaped leaves that radiate from a central point. True American chestnuts have reddish stems and petioles and long, narrow, canoe-shaped leaves with saw-toothed edges that turn yellow in fall. The burs, which hold the nuts, are green and dense with vicious, inch-long needles, while horse chestnut burs are brown and sparsely covered with quarter-inch prickers.

> **True American chestnuts have reddish stems... and leaves with saw-toothed edges that turn yellow in fall.**

The Massachusetts Chapter already has found more blooming-age trees than they dreamed existed. In 2000, one of the only known groves of chestnuts in the region was discovered right in the heart of Boston, in the Stony Brook Reservation overlooking Turtle Pond. It had four blooming adults located close enough to pollinate each other.

It's not known whether the state's fruitful chestnuts are regrowths, from old roots, or new trees. However, since all die of the blight soon after reaching blooming age (except for trees growing in isolation), breeding them with Chinese chestnuts is the only real hope.

"It may be false hopes," says volunteer Frank A. Howard as he tramps through the Stony Brook woods. "But I've seen the peregrine falcon come back, and the eagle come back. There's lots of success stories." ❁

Below: Harvesting the scarce wild American chestnuts that were previously bagged to protect them from squirrels until maturity. (Boston Globe photo/ Tom Landers)

WHO DOES YOUR GARDEN GROW?

THIS FALL, WHILE 'ALMA POTCHKE' AND 'PATRICIA BALLARD' are blushing bright pink, 'Ann Folkard' and 'Claridge Dulce' will be turning red with the cold. You can count on 'David,' 'Miss Lingard,' and 'Caroline van den Berg' to put on a second performance if you deadheaded them faithfully.

As you survey your garden with quiet satisfaction, though, one question tugs at you. Who are these people?

All of us have landscapes full of plants named after people we've never heard of otherwise. They're among the mysteries of the garden. Whoever Miss Lingard once was – wife, mistress or pet cat – she's a phlox now.

There are also flowers named after celebrities, of course, which enjoy sales boosts from borrowed star power, such as a miniature daylily named after Grand Ole Opry comedienne Minnie Pearl, or a full-blown, old-fashioned peony christened after the sumptuous Edwardian actress Sarah Bernhardt.

Though names such as 'Gina Lollobrigida' and 'Cary Grant' have brought sex appeal to the rose garden, royalty still reigns in that particular bed. 'Prince Charles' is a crimson Bourbon rose, while 'Diana, Princess of Wales,' as well as 'Princess Margaret' and 'Queen Elizabeth,' are all pink. ('Queen Elizabeth' is the best performer.) 'Julia Child' is a new yellow rose that looks particularly scrumptious.

In this age of celebrity, however, it's perhaps surprising how many plants are named after regular people who then become part of our backyards, if not our lives. For instance, the most popular daphne is named 'Carol Mackie,' after the woman who was lucky enough to discover this silver-edged mutation of the burkwoodii daphne growing in her New Jersey garden.

The giant sea holly Eryngium giganteum was dubbed 'Miss Wilmott's Ghost' because in the early 1900s, noted gardener Ellen Wilmott would scatter its seeds around gardens she visited. The next year, the gardens' owners would be either admiring or weeding out 4-foot-tall biennial sea hollies. In either case, their friends would say something like, "I see Miss Wilmott was here."

Some plants are named for more than one person. The popular Hosta sieboldiana 'Frances Williams' is named after a collector who spotted a seedling of H. sieboldiana variety elegans in 1936 growing at Bristol Nurseries in Connecticut.

The Latinized part of the name of this plant, and many others such as towering Hydrangea paniculata 'Siebold Grandiflora,' refers to Philipp Franz Balthasar von Siebold. He was the first European to introduce the wild plants from Japan. While today's breeders pick the name for garden cultivars (which often go out of fashion), plant explorers and their patrons got in on the ground floor, lending their names to species, or even a whole genus of plants, the bedrock taxonomic classification.

Above: 'John F. Kennedy' rose. (Photo courtesy of Jackson & Perkins)

Above: 'Bela Lugosi' daylily. Left: 'Paris d'Yves St. Laurent' rose. (Photos courtesy of www.parkseed.com)

Most of the human names in your garden trace back to plant breeders and their families. Ernest Ballard of Colwall, England, named a cultivar of asters for every member of his family, including 'Patricia.' Geranium 'Ann Folkard' is a natural hybrid that occurred in 1973 between G. procurrens and G. psilostemon in the garden of the Rev. O.G. Folkard, who named it after his wife. 'Claridge Dulce,' a pink geranium with dark veins, is named after its originator.

You might be growing a 'Merrill' magnolia, named for Elmer Drew Merrill, a director at Harvard's Arnold Arboretum, or a 'Donald Wyman' crab apple, named for an esteemed horticulturist who also worked there.

Though thousands of varieties of irises, daylilies, daffodils, tulips, hostas and rhododendrons have been named after people, only a tiny fraction of these enjoy the distinctiveness, vigor and promotion it takes to make it to your backyard. Breeding a plant and building up stock for sale is typically a 20-year project.

'Anne Frank' was a popular white tulip two decades ago but is no longer available because the breeding stock developed disease. There can never be another 'Anne Frank' tulip. The yellow 'John F. Kennedy' tulip and the giant red 'General Eisenhower' tulip (so named by the Dutch for the general's efforts liberating Holland during World War II) are still going strong, though, and a pink 'Hillary Clinton' tulip was introduced a few years back. ❁

GARDENER'S WEEK 1

Hydrangeas: Don't cut down hydrangeas with colored flowers or they won't bloom in the spring, though you can cut off the flower heads for neatness. You can cut down 'Annabelle,' a popular 3-foot hydrangea with giant white flower heads in summer. If your blue hydrangea fails to bloom each summer, try covering it completely with a mound of bark mulch to protect the buds. Uncover it at the end of March.

Hoses: Unhook and drain garden hoses completely, roll them up and store them off the ground.

Irrigation system: If you have an automatic system, shut down the timer. If the timer has a digital display, switch to the "rain" setting on the controller. If it has a dial, like an analog clock face, or a pump is wired to the timer, turn off the power to save electricity.

Leaves: They're not really harmful unless they're thick enough to suffocate what's underneath, so you don't have to bother raking leaves out of beds or between shrubs. But lawns have to be kept reasonably clear.

Shrubs and trees: Dig deciduous woodies to relocate them after they have lost their leaves (or in early spring). To move a shrub, you have to dig out the rootball, which could weigh more than 100 pounds. Get a big tarp. If the shrub is small, pry it out with a shovel-sized garden fork, inserted and levered from all sides. For larger shrubs, dig a deep trench around the outside of the rootball and put the dirt on the tarp. Then pry the underside of the rootball loose, lifting and rolling it onto the tarp alongside. Slide the dirt you dug out back into the hole. Drag the shrub to its new location, lifting it as little as possible unless you have help. Replant it so the top of the rootball is level with the surrounding soil. If the shrub doesn't have a single trunk but a bunch of stems rising from ground level, you can divide it like a perennial to get more.

Weeds: This is a good time to spot and eradicate perennial weedy vines such as deadly nightshade or bittersweet that hide in hedges or shrubberies, but have leaves that turn a different fall color.

KNOW YOUR TERMS

HARDY BULBS: Tulips and other winter-proof flowers planted in the fall to bloom in the spring.

NON-HARDY BULBS: Dahlias, gladiolas, elephant ears and other tropicals planted in late spring to sprout in summer. They're also called "summer bulbs."

Above photos, left to right:

White-tailed deer

Native wood aster

Bird feeder in maple tree

Evergreen Thuja 'Green Giant'

(Boston Globe photos/ Mark Wilson, Pam Berry; evergreen photo courtesy of www.parkseed. com)

GARDENER'S WEEK 2

Bulbs: Keep planting hardy bulbs with a shovel and lifting non-hardy kinds with a garden fork for indoor winter storage.

Cleanup: Store lawn furniture and garden art that might be damaged by spending winter outdoors. Process fallen branches through a chipper for free landscaping mulch.

Composting: What should you compost? Perennial tops you've cut back, dying potted plants and annuals along with their root balls, leaves, grass cuttings, straw, chipped brush, sawdust, pine needles, weeds, vegetable and fruit wastes, seaweed, eggshells, coffee grounds and paper filters, teabags, and any manure that isn't from carnivores such as dogs or cats. You can also compost shredded paper and cardboard, including newspaper, paper towels, paper plates and paper bags. (But don't compost dairy products, meat, fat or grease, cooked foods with sauces, bones, peanut butter, mature weed seeds, diseased plants, weeds that spread by roots and runners, vines, whole branches, dog and cat manure, or kitty litter.) Tiny organisms will convert your refuse into a form living plants can use. These molds and fungi like to have moisture and oxygen and will work faster if the pile is kept moist as a wrung-out sponge and aerated. A bottom layer of coarse material such as corn stalks or wood chips will help provide air. Some people turn their compost piles with a pitchfork occasionally so the bottom material ends up on top. This not only aerates the pile, but puts the older, ready-to-use compost on top where you can get at it. When it looks like rich brown soil, crumbles in your fingers, and smells earthy and sweet, it's ready to use for planting, spreading over garden beds or potting indoor plants. Having multiple compost piles in different stages of readiness enables you to have one pile to add new refuse to and another pile with compost ready for use.

Garden journal: While you're still working outdoors and your memory is fresh, take time to record lessons and ideas that you want to act on next year.

Tidy Choice: Decide if you want to postpone finishing cleanup until next spring. The uncut garden will provide cover and food for birds, who especially like the seed heads of zinnias, coreopsis, rudbeckias, agastaches and cone flowers.

Trees and shrubs: Protect young fruit trees from gnawing mice and sun scald by wrapping the base of trunks with commercial tree wrap or metal tree guards you can make from 18-inch-tall cylinders of mesh hardware cloth.

TOP 10
Things about gardening in New England:

10 **Frederick Law Olmsted. He invented landscape architecture here.**

9 **Lots of plant societies and distinguished botanical gardens.**

8 **Old apple trees. Johnny Appleseed was born here.**

7 **No fire ants and very little kudzu. It gets too cold.**

6 **Great family-owned nurseries.**

5 **Ocean climate. Mountain climate. Take your pick.**

4 **Rain. Whenever.**

3 **Gardeners really know what they're talking about, mostly.**

2 **Four (or five) seasons.**

1 **One of them is fall.**

GARDENER'S WEEK 3

Broad-leaved evergreens:
Mulch the roots with oak leaves if you have them.

Cleanup: Clean and store any remaining garden furniture, stakes, cages and trellises. Store pesticides and fertilizer in a dry, locked area that's labeled for dangerous chemicals. Give your newly exposed beds and borders one last weeding, but don't compost weeds that have gone to seed. Pry out deep-rooted perennial weeds such a pokeweed and dock with a long, narrow weeding tool such as an asparagus fork. Add their roots, which are a good source of phosphorus, to the compost pile.

Draining outdoor faucets:
Inside the house is a shut-off for each exterior faucet, usually just on the other side of the basement wall from the outside faucet. Shut off each of these from inside the basement, then open the outside faucet to drain any remaining water. Back inside, look for the vent on the bottom of each valve. Put a bucket under each and then unscrew with pliers. Remove the half-inch metal cap and `O' ring inside the bottom of the shut-off, using a pin to break the vacuum. Water will drain out from that 5-foot section of pipe between the inside and outside faucet; otherwise it can freeze and burst inside the wall, causing damage that's expensive to repair.

Iris: Iris borer eggs winter over in old bearded iris foliage, so cut down the foliage and dispose of it.

Lawn: Finish liming and fertilizing. Rake up lawn leaves and add them to the compost pile. Mow the lawn for the last time at a height of 1 1/2 to 2 inches. Though cuttings are usually left on the lawn to decompose, this last time rake them up and add them to the compost pile to help prevent snow mold over the winter. Don't rake new lawns until spring.

Trees and shrubs: Water newly planted woodies until the ground freezes. Fertilize established plants with 10-10-10.

Above photos, left to right:

Mulch with shredded leaves

Chrysanthemums

'Autumn Monkshood'

Gourds

Wild turkey (yes, they're making a comeback; attract them by spreading cracked corn on the ground)

(Boston Globe photos/ Pat Greenhouse, John Blanding, Tom Landers; chrysanthemums courtesy of Proven Winners® – www.proven-winners.com)

GARDENER'S WEEK 4

Christmas tree: Finding the right tree is important, but finding the right tree stand is even more so. Spurn teeny tree stands. A Christmas tree can drink up to a gallon of water a day; the key to its long life is to find a stand that holds two or three gallons of water and keep it constantly full. After you buy your tree, store it in a shady, cool area outdoors. The last thing you do before you set it up is cut an inch off the butt to expose fresh wood, which is immediately immersed in warm water before it can dry out. If the freshly cut end of the tree dries out after it's been set up (horrors!) it will lose the ability to drink and soon be a goner unless you recut the butt again. And that's pretty hard to do once the ornaments are on.

Garden pond: If you plan to keep fish in it over the winter, keep the pump running and arrange its intake to draw water from a foot above the pond bottom. If fish are not a factor, when the water surface develops persistent ice, shut off and disconnect your submersible pump, clean it and store it in a dry place until spring. Then drain all lines and the filter, and clean the filter pads. Even if you don't have fish, clean out excess sludge and debris from the water.

Ornamental pots: Many pots now are so durable they're able to survive the winter without cracking, even if they remain filled with soil. High-fired stoneware will not break. Test the quality by tapping it; high-fired pottery has a higher-pitched sound with a ring to it, while less durable, earthenware, low-fired pots have a dull sound. The more expensive pots that look like lead or terra cotta can stay out all winter, too. If you want to ensure the safety of costly pots over the winter, dump their soil in the compost pile, wash and sterilize them with a 10 percent bleach solution, and let them dry in the sun on a warm day before storing indoors or in a garage or shed. If you don't have storage space, turn them upside down and cover them so the drainage holes won't admit rain and the pots won't be exposed to degradation by sunlight.

Potted plants: If you have hardy perennials or woody plants growing in pots that you plan to leave outside all winter, their chances of survival will be enhanced if you bury each pot up to its rim and cover the root zone with mulch.

Roses: Mound 4 inches of soil around the trunks of roses to protect them from thaws and freezes. Don't dig up the soil from around the roses to do this or you may expose their roots. In the spring, remove the mound by spreading the compost over the root areas for extra nutrients. Prune ramblers and climbers and fasten them firmly to their supports so they don't get whipped around by winter winds. Clean up the rose garden and bag any diseased leaves – don't add them to the compost pile.

Structural maintenance: Repair greenhouses, trellises, potting sheds and cold frames for use next year.

KNOW YOUR TERMS

pH: A measurement of acidity on a scale of 1 to 14. Soil with a pH greater than 7 is alkaline. Though some plants, such as lawn grass and lilacs prefer a slightly alkaline pH, most plants prefer a slightly acidic pH of 5.5 to 6.5.

PLANT OF THE MONTH

Sedum (Sedum).

These diverse, well-behaved plants require almost nothing but sunlight to thrive. The hybrid 'Autumn Joy' (below) looks like neat green heads of broccoli in summer. In fall it produces pink star-like flowers that attract butterflies. In winter the flat seed head turns coppery red.

(Below: Boston Globe photo/ Wendy Maeda. Right: Sedum 'Postman's Pride' photo courtesy of www.parkseed.com.)

MR. HOLLY JOLLY CHRISTMAS

PEOPLE HAVE TOLD BILL CANNON THAT HE RESEMBLES SANTA CLAUS, with his rosy smile and full silver beard. And his choice of hobby does little to dispel the impression. Though there are a lot of Christmas tree farms in New England, Cannon owns one of the region's only holly farms.

This is the perfect time to prune holly trees and bushes, and Cannon uses the annual prunings from his collection of 300 holly species and cultivars to make unique Christmas wreaths for local florists near his home. Though holly sprigs need to be in water indoors, they'll last through the holidays outdoors, especially if the cut ends are inserted into soil in a planter. Cannon sticks his holly clippings into rings of damp sphagnum moss to keep them fresh.

Everyone should plant a holly bush. Actually, two bushes. Hollies, unlike most plants, have genders. Only the females produce berries, optimally when there's a male growing within 300 feet for pollination. Holly is a wonderful plant that, once established, tolerates shade, drought and neglect (except for planting in a spot where water collects).

Left: Santa… er, Bill Cannon makes wreaths from a mix of homegrown varieties that include winterberry, English holly and blue holly. (Boston Globe photo/ John Tlumacki)

So why is so much of New England planted with evergreen rhododendrons instead of hollies? Alas, hollies have a tragic flaw. Like hydrangeas, most of the best types get throttled by our harsh winters.

If you live on comparatively balmy Cape Cod, where Cannon has his farm, you live in holly heaven. The southern New England coast is also good holly territory. If I lived there I would plant a dozen types, including at least one English holly (Ilex aquifolium) shaped like a Christmas tree with variegated yellow-edged green leaves and lots of red berries.

But if you live north of Boston or inland, your choices are more limited.

Fortunately, there's one terrific hybrid strain of evergreen holly that does well here, the Merserve (pronounced "mer zev") holly. Available at every good local nursery, these patented plants were bred 50 years ago by a well-to-do New York housewife named Elizabeth Merserve, who crossed wild hollies from Siberia with many other species to produce the first evergreen holly shrubs with red berries that can be grown in large areas of New England. They also resist disease and tolerate shade. "You can't beat them. They're foolproof," says Cannon. They're sometimes called "blue hollies" because of their shiny blue-green foliage, and have names such as 'Blue Princess' for the female and 'Blue Prince' for her consort. (Those two are Carey Award winners.) If you want a pyramidal holly tree instead of a holly bush, plant the Merserve variety 'Dragon Lady' in full sun.

Also hardy here is long stalk holly (Ilex pendunculosa), which has red berries that hang like cherries, and American holly (Ilex opaca), which will grow into a 40-foot evergreen tree in a sunny but sheltered location in much of coastal New England.

American holly is a native woodland plant though not many survive in the wild because people "shred the trees collecting their red berries," says Cannon. These trees are disease prone and may require spraying in mid-May and mid-June with Merit to kill leafminers. If the berries won't turn red, you have berry midges and should dispose of all the green berries.

The hardiest available evergreen holly is a native shrub called inkberry (Ilex glabra). But Cannon says deer like it and it has black berries, as does the similar Japanese holly (Ilex crenata).

If you live in the Berkshires, there's only one holly for you, and it's not an evergreen. Though the native winterberry (Ilex verticillata) loses its leaves, the bright orange and red berries stand out even better and intensive breeding has increased their size and quantity. This is one holly that does like damp locations and you can find it growing wild near swamps. Cannon's favorite varieties are 'Winter Red,' 'Winter Gold' and 'Maryland Beauty.'

As a member of the Holly Society of America, Cannon knows almost every new and improved variety in the horticultural pipeline. He recommends protecting newly planted hollies from wind damage their first winter by surrounding them with stakes and a wall of burlap. "You don't need to cover the top, just the sides," he says, and he doesn't bother spraying with an anti-desiccant because he's not convinced it helps.

Other tips for holly care include mulching with pine needles or bark, and fertilizing in both April and June with Hollytone or a similar fertilizer. Cannon fertilizes with Milorganite, derived from sewer sludge, because he thinks the smell repels deer. ❀

Far left: Merserve holly.
Left: Winterberry is a holly that loses its leaves but is gaining in popularity.

(All photos courtesy of Proven Winners® – www.provenwinners.com)

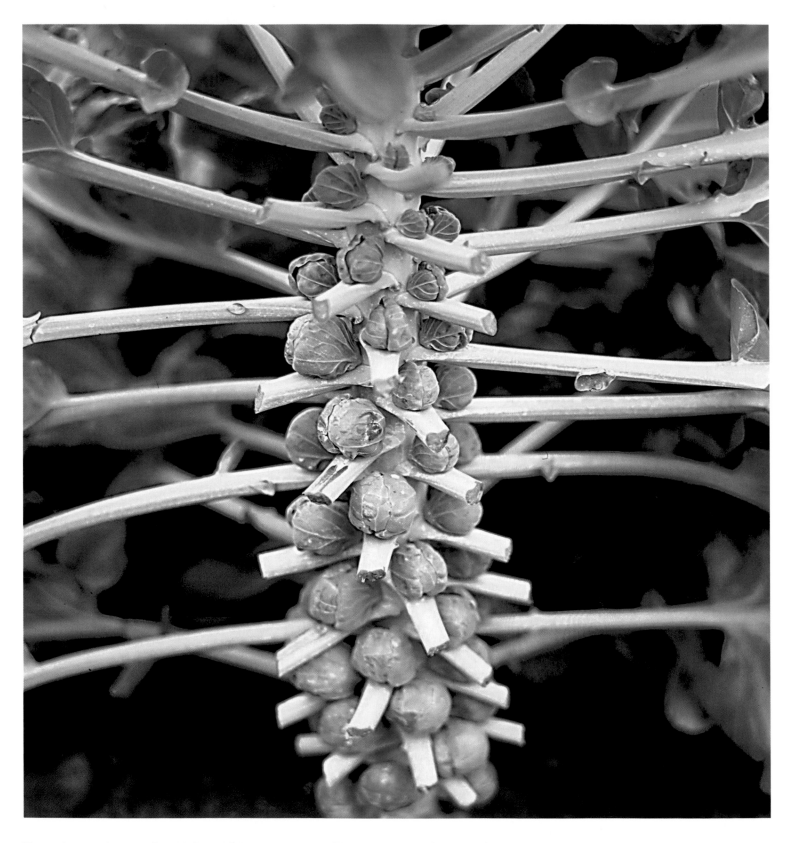

Brussels sprouts are a frost-tolerant late-season crop. (Photo courtesy of www.parkseed.com)

Blue holly is a mainstay of the winter landscape. (Photo courtesy of www.parkseed.com)

CLASSIC TASHA TUDOR

I MET HER IN 1994.

There she was, turning to greet me in her cottage kitchen with its hand-pump sink and wood stove. She was swathed in layers of handmade clothes that covered her collarbone, her wrists, her ankles. She was regal, not smiling, a bit frail. And barefoot.

I remember Tasha Tudor's striped lavender dress, patterned like old wallpaper. It had a fitted bodice and flowing skirt, a handknit collar of brown wool almost as large as a shawl. Her long silver hair was knotted in a kerchief. She looked like a frontierswoman.

"I never read newspapers," she announced with a sideways glance meant to measure reaction from her journalist houseguest. "I just use them to line bird cages."

It was that kind of lunch date. I loved every minute of it.

Chances are you know Tasha Tudor, even if you think you don't. She's the woman who painted the delicate illustrations for the "The Secret Garden" and more than 80 other children's books. Her flower-entwined borders and Victorian tykes have graced untold pages of calendars and stationery and launched countless imitations.

Though Tudor, now in her nineties, fiercely guards her privacy, her life in the hills of southern Vermont is enough like her art to have inspired several evocative coffee table books, including "Tasha Tudor's Garden" (Houghton Mifflin) photographed by Richard Brown and written by Tovah Martin.

Shunning television, radio and modern culture in general, Tudor has chosen to replicate a favorite decade in her home, garden and clothing: that decade is the 1830s. She's a woman who prefers to weave on a loom, make her own dolls, and cook (gourmet) on a wood stove. When not busy painting, Tudor has spent countless hours fussing over her fancy fowl, maintaining her greenhouse, stacking firewood and planting her huge garden almost single-handedly.

"I've always lived this way," she told me over our lunch of homemade chicken soup, homebaked bread, homegrown raspberries and tea in handle-less cups. "We didn't have electricity until my youngest child was 5 . . . I felt so sorry for the hippies who thought the quiet life was just the thing. They were not ready for chopping wood and taking care of animals. I was raised this way. It was nothing to me."

Though Tudor's house and garden look as if they've been on this Vermont hilltop for 200 years, the truth is closer to 30. Her brown cottage is a replica of a 1740 New Hampshire farmhouse that she liked. It was constructed using only hand tools by her son, Seth.

Left to right: Tasha Tudor has chosen mid-19th century New England as the template for her life and art. Here she picks sweetpeas, works on an illustration and takes time out for one of her beloved Corgis. (Photos courtesy of Richard W. Brown/ "Tasha Tudor's Garden," Houghton Mifflin)

Tudor has followed in the footsteps of her parents, who were born to privileged New England families and also turned their backs on convention. Her father, William Starling Burgess, was a Marblehead-based yacht designer who devised inventions with Buckminster Fuller that never quite fulfilled expectations. The same is true of the career of her mother, Rosamond Tudor, a portrait painter who resettled in Greenwich Village after the couple divorced when Tudor was 9.

She was then sent to live with theatrical family friends in Redding, CT, who raised her with their own children to read aloud from Shakespeare and put on amateur plays with costumes, tickets and painted scenery. Tudor fell in love with country living and the world of imagination.

In 1938 she published her first children's book, "Pumpkin Moonshine," and married a well-meaning but ineffectual "suburbanite" who worked at farming to please her, but never managed to support the family.

She divorced him, and with four children to support, credited "the wolf at the door" for helping her realize a commercial potential that exceeded her parents' and is rare among artists. Canny as well as hard-working, she sold her original drawings, negotiated smart contracts and even got Life magazine to photograph the wedding of two

of her handcrafted dolls.

Tudor raised her family in a rundown 1790s house in New Hampshire purchased with royalties from her illustrated "Mother Goose." The home had no electricity or running water, but 17 rooms and 450 acres of land. Several decades ago she sold it to move to this more remote location, taking her antique plumbing fixtures and favorite garden plants with her.

"I never cared for that house like I did this one," she remarked with typical candor. "I took all my peonies. I took rhododendrons. The road up here was just a path then." The plants came in by wheelbarrow, supplies by backpack. "It was good for the figure."

Now when the leaves fall, I think of Tudor squirreling away the remarkable cornucopia of her garden (which is not open to public tours). I see potatoes lying in baskets in her cellar. Carrots, beets and turnips are down there, too, layered with sand, waiting just to be sprinkled occasionally with water to help them keep. Far below the greenhouse and her stone terraces of perennials, I imagine the vegetable garden lies waiting for next year, surrounded by a neat square of evergreen hedge. ❄

GARDENER'S WEEK 1

Living Christmas trees: Though widely sold for planting outdoors after Christmas, these dug up trees with balled and burlaped roots are inconvenient and have only about a 50-50 survival rate in New England, so they may not save you landscaping dollars. If you plan to get one, dig your planting hole now and fill it with leaves and cover the excavated soil with mulch or store it where it will not freeze. Then cover the hole with a tarp until planting time to keep the ground from freezing. Because live Christmas trees won't survive if left indoors more than 10 days, wait until close to Christmas Eve to buy your tree and plant it immediately after New Year's. The tree will probably weigh about 200 pounds with its rootball, so bring plenty of muscle power and have a dolly waiting at home. Bring the tree inside in stages, with a day spent in the breezeway or garage. Keep the roots moist at all times.

Evergreen decorations: Broad-leaved evergreens have a tendency to dry out more quickly than needled evergreens, though a few stems can provide variety. Holly stems need to be in water when used indoors. Crush the ends of woody stems with a hammer and place them in a bucket of water that's hot but comfortable to the touch, allowing three hours of soaking before using. Cut 6- to 9-inch lengths for making wreaths. Use boxwood, hemlock, Scotch pine, arborvitae, laurel, chamaecyparis, spruce or balsam for the outdoors, where they'll stay green for months without water. Don't use white pine, spruce or balsam indoors unless they'll be in water. Scotch pine, arborvitae, chamaecyparis, laurel and boxwood are fine indoors without water. Avoid using hemlock indoors, as the needles shed.

Winter pruning: You can do this anytime trees are leafless. Prune in stages. First remove dead or diseased wood, and then proceed to removing weak and crossed stems (which can rub against each other). Then shape the plant. All cuts should be at an angle slanting slightly above and away from a bud or lower branch. Prune hedges, especially evergreen ones, so they are narrower at the top than at the base to help prevent winter winds and snow from breaking the hedge by splaying the branches. Use shears to start cutting from the bottom and work your way up so the clippings don't get in your way.

Vegetables: Pick kale and other hardy greens being grown in cold frames. Heavily mulch root crops such as rutabagas, which can continue to be harvested until the ground freezes. Bales of salt marsh hay are ideal for this.

Above photo:

Patronizing a local farm where you can cut or select your own Christmas tree will help insure its freshness and long life. This also makes a great family outing.

(Boston Globe photo/ Tom Landers)

GARDENER'S WEEK 2

Christmas trees: This is the biggest week for buying Christmas trees, but what kind of tree should you chose? Balsam and Fraser firs are aromatic and hold their needles well. Balsam fir is New England's answer to lavender, with blunt, glossy green needles about an inch long that smell so good they are sometimes used to stuff little pillows. White and Scotch pines also hold their needles and are fragrant, but white pines have weak branches, so you need to use lightweight ornaments to avoid drooping. A white spruce can shed its needles after it dries out, whereas blue spruce holds its needles well and people like the bluish tint, which looks especially pretty when this tree is decked with blue lights. But blue spruce smells musty, and the needles are so sharp that you need to wear thick gloves to handle or decorate the tree. Hemlock is better used for outdoor decorations because it dries out indoors.

The cutting: In addition to ensuring freshness, you'll support local farming and probably save money with a family expedition to a choose-and-cut tree farm. When you go to cut your tree, choose a day with temperatures below 50 degrees if that's convenient; trees suffer more trauma on warm days. If you buy your tree already cut from a retail lot, tap the butt of the tree on the ground and don't buy it if a lot of needles fall off. Also, a fresh tree will bend instead of break. To find a list of nearby Christmas tree retailers, enter your ZIP code at www.RealChristmasTrees.org, the National Christmas Tree Association website.

Deer: Evergreen arborvitae, yew, ivy, rhododendron, vinca and euonymus are among deer's favorite winter foods. So if you have a problem with browsers, wrap individual shrubs in the black netting used to keep birds off berry bushes, because deer don't like to bite into it. To protect trees and tall evergreens such as cedars from browsing, wrap them in sturdy multi-use plastic (wire style) fencing that is at least 6.5 feet tall with a grid of an inch or less so deer can't stick their noses through. (For sale occasionally at Home Depot stores, this can also be ordered from U.S. Fence at www.us-fence.com; 800-455-5167.) You can also spray evergreens with any of the wide assortment of products that repel deer through smell and taste (sources include Deerbusters at www.deerbusters.com; 301-694-6072).

Outdoor lighting: This is a time when we admire outdoor holiday lights. Give some thought to what you can do to permanently improve the quality of your landscape illumination.

Table decorations: The front yard can yield both unexpected and traditional holiday greenery, including firm-needled spruce, clusters of pyracantha berries, ivy, cedar branches, sprigs of viburnum berries, the last of the crab apples, elegant sprays of andromeda and, of course, holly.

Trees: To anchor young trees against root-rocking by wind, tie each trunk to two or three stakes with old pantyhose that will have some give.

Vegetables: If any carrots are still in the garden but not mulched, dig them up and store them in a cool garage or basement. Harvest Brussels sprouts and cabbage, roots and all, and they will keep for weeks. You can leave parsnips in the ground all winter and harvest them in early spring.

GARDENER'S WEEK 3

Birds: Share the holidays with all forms of life. Set up a feeder now, where you can see it from the window, and fill it with feed each evening, since the birds probably get up before you do. The red male cardinal is a favorite wild bird at Christmastime; fill your feeder with black-oil sunflower seeds to attract him. Plan to continue feeding at least until April. Once birds become habituated to your feeder, you shouldn't discontinue until they have alternative sources of food available, such as spring insects.

Centerpieces: For inexpensive flower arrangements, combine red carnations with evergreen sprigs from your backyard, especially those with finely textured needles such as pines or firs.

Christmas tree: Remember, it's a plant; treat it as you would a bouquet of flowers. Christmas trees are longest lasting if you cut them yourself, recut the stems before putting them in

water, place them in a cool spot and keep the water container topped off. It will drink up to a gallon of water a day. Set the tree up in a spot away from heat sources such as stoves, heaters, fireplaces and TV sets, as well as drafts. Don't decorate with tinsel, spray paint or anything else that will inhibit composting and recycling.

Cyclamen: These long-flowering plants come in cool holiday colors such as maroon, pink and white. Buy plants with lots of buds under the leaves and put them in bright but indirect light in a cool room (ideally, 65 degrees). Water from the bottom and fertilize with high-phosphorus plant food every two weeks. When flowering ceases in March, let the soil dry out between waterings. Put the plant outside for the summer in direct sun and repot in late summer when new leaves appear, making sure the top half of the corm is above soil level.

Gift wrap: Try using fresh flowers from bouquets or evergreen twigs or berries cut from the garden to accent last-minute wrapping projects.

Grapevine wreaths: These are a snap. Cut the longest piece you can, then put your foot at one end and twist it around itself as though you're winding a hose. It's most flexible when you first cut it. You don't even have to tie it with wire; once you use enough of it, it interlocks by itself.

Office plants: If you're leaving them for the holidays, water them thoroughly, group them together in a bright window, and make a tent around them with a dry-cleaning bag. Water them as soon as you return.

Poinsettias: These require very little care. They aren't fussy about light or temperature and only ask that you water them when they're dry. Poinsettias used to drop their leaves after the holidays, but the discovery

of a sturdy mutation in 1963 now means they keep blooming almost indefinitely. Temperatures of 65 to 70 degrees are ideal to prolong the bright red bracts.

Vegetables: You can still harvest Brussels sprouts, cabbage, carrots, parsnips and salsify that have been mulched with bales of straw in the garden.

Above photos, left to right:

Christmas wreath of evergreen magnolia leaves

Deer

Kale

Winterberry

Miscanthus seedheads

(Boston Globe photos/ Tom Landers, Mark Wilson, Jonathan Wiggs; winterberry and miscanthus courtesy of Proven Winners® – www.proven-winners.com)

GARDENER'S WEEK 4

Azaleas: If the buds on these indoor Christmas plants turn brown and papery and don't open, or the leaves turn brown and fall, increase watering (with warm water), move them to a cooler location (the floor is the coolest spot in any room) and try a humidifier. If the leaves turn yellow with green veins, use an acid-based houseplant fertilizer with iron.

Bulbs: If someone has given you loose hyacinth or paperwhite narcissus bulbs, set them on top of a bowl of pebbles. Fill the container with water until it just touches the base of the bulbs and place it in a well-lit window. The bulb roots will grow into the pebbles to anchor the plants, which will sprout and bloom over a period of several months if the proper water level is maintained. Discard the bulbs after blooming.

Christmas trees: Once the holidays are over, recycle your tree rather than putting it out in one of those big plastic trash bags. It can be chipped and shredded into mulch for your garden. Or you can cut off the boughs and place them on your perennial beds for added protection against spring thaws. You can also place it near a birdfeeder to give birds shelter from wind and predators. Be sure to remove all decorations, lights, tinsel and any nails used in the base of the trunk.

Decorations: Replace plant material that is looking tired. After Christmas, use more white candles and flowers in place of red ones.

Living Christmas trees: Keep the rootball constantly moist. The fewer days it spends in the house, the greater its chances of survival. By New Year's Day, move it to a chilly breezeway or garage for 24 hours to help acclimate it to the weather change. Then plant the rootball in your previously excavated hole. It's better to plant it a little too high than a little too deep. After filling in the soil, cover the planting area with leaves and mulch. Water immediately with several buckets of water, and keep watering it this way all winter except when the ground is frozen hard. It's a lot of work! If your tree lives, you have a right to feel proud.

Potpourris: Keeping a pot of water containing a cinnamon stick and cloves over low heat on the stove will put fragrant moisture in the air to help both plants and humans breathe.

Spring garden catalogs: It's hard to believe how soon these start to arrive. Publishers are hoping to gain your attention while you're on vacation.

Amaryllis (Hippaestrum).

It's always miraculous to watch the foot-tall stalk emerge from this large bulb, followed by three to six gigantic flowers in Christmas red, hot pink or frosted white. Fertilize every two weeks and don't water for three months in the fall to get it to rebloom.

(Photo courtesy of Netherlands Flower Bulb Information Center)

JANUARY

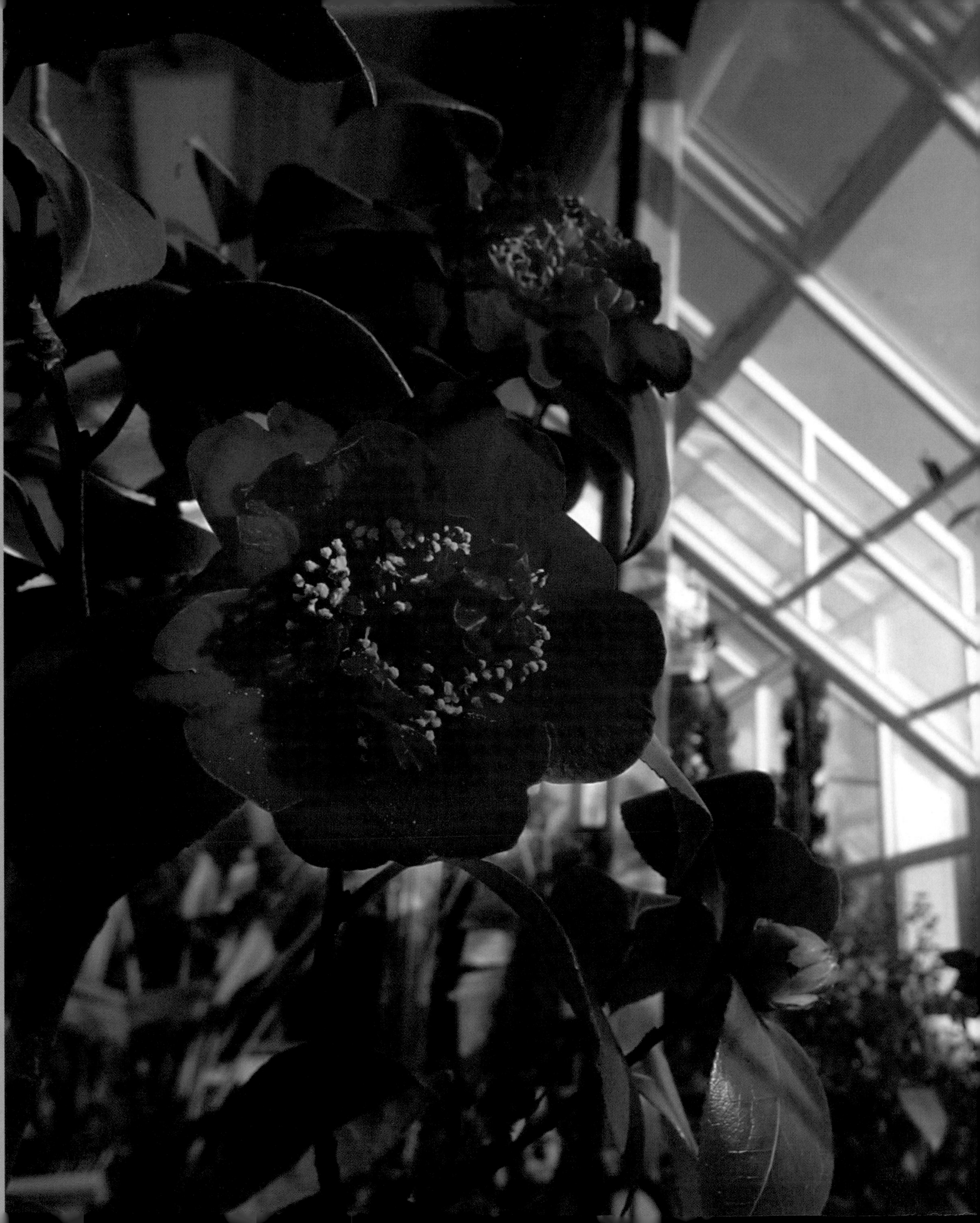

IT'S TIME TO COME INSIDE

ON SUNNY WINTER DAYS, JAMES JONES FREQUENTLY SETTLES INTO one of three unheated homemade greenhouses surrounding his house in Lexington, MA. There he reads, does crossword puzzles and enjoys the lush scents of blooming narcissus and daphne odora. Temperatures inside the greenhouses are comfortable in sunshine, the retired scientist says, "and if it's cloudy, I just don't go out there."

Once a sign of wealth, home greenhouses have become a more casual pleasure, available in every price range.

"There're probably twice as many options as there were five years ago because there are a lot more manufacturers," explains Charley Yaw, president of Charley's Greenhouse & Garden in Mt. Vernon, WA, one of the largest sellers of greenhouses and supplies. The new diversity is largely powered by the rising use and falling price of an insulated plastic glazing material called polycarbonate, which has gained about 90 percent of the home greenhouse market in the last 10 years.

Left: Camellias, once great status symbols in New England, at the historic Lyman Estate greenhouses in Waltham, MA. (Boston Globe photo/ Tom Herde)

GREENHOUSE FAQ

HOW DO I CHOOSE A GREENHOUSE SITE?
It should receive at least six hours of direct sunlight during the winter months.

HOW MUCH DOES IT COST?
A sturdy, permanent, free-standing greenhouse 6 feet by 8 feet can cost less than $1,000.

HOW BIG SHOULD IT BE?
Six feet by 8 feet is the minimum. The larger it is, the easier it is to keep an even temperature because smaller structures heat up and cool down faster. Eight by 12 feet will give you enough room for a sitting area.

SHOULD IT BE FREE-STANDING OR ATTACHED?
Free-standing is usually cheaper and more adaptable. However, lean-tos are closer to power and water sources and gain heat from the house, while providing some home insulation in return.

WILL I NEED TO HEAT IT?
An unheated, free-standing greenhouse will stay only 10 degrees warmer than the outdoors. An attached greenhouse with passive solar techniques such as heat sinks will stay much warmer.

DOES IT NEED ELECTRICITY AND WATER?
Not necessarily. There are solar vent openers and louvered windows for air intake and escape, but electricity will power circulating fans and lights. For watering, you can use a covered reservoir that will double as an energy-saving heat sink.

Above: The pansies get plenty of pampering at this greenhouse in Newton, MA. (Boston Globe photo/ David L. Ryan)

"By far the best choice for the hobbyist," says Yaw. "Polycarbonate glazing has made an energy-efficient greenhouse available to anyone who wants one."

Jennifer Brindisi, a retired earth science teacher, is one. In 2003 she added a 12-by-8-foot greenhouse from Sunglow Solar Greenhouses, also in Washington state, along the south wall of her Massachusetts home. She chose corrugated clear plastic polycarbonate that came pre-cut for self-assembly. The $4,000 price tag included electricity for lights, fans and heat, plus a contractor to dig a 3-foot-deep foundation filled with almost five tons of crushed rock to retain warmth. A 55-gallon water drum was included to moderate temperatures. Brindisi admits that, for her, function came before classic beauty.

The current revolution in home greenhouse technology emphasizes solar energy techniques and the inexpensive but efficient plastic shells of polycarbonate and acrylic fiberglass. Even antique greenhouses are getting updated. Anne Allen recently replaced the glass panes of the century-old New England greenhouse she inherited from her grandmother with acrylic fiberglass. "The glass slipped and every year it had to be regrouted," she explains.

Some people still go low-tech. One New Englander spent only a few hundred dollars to convert the front porch of her circa 1920 home into a growing space for her collection of 70 orchids. It had baseboard heating and its own thermostat, so she bought a humidifier, instruments to measure humidity (kept at 50 percent), two rotating fans to circulate the air, and racks to put the plants on.

PLACES TO VISIT

New England is blessed with many professional greenhouses open to the public.
Here are just a few. Call for directions, hours and admission fees.

**LYMAN CONSERVATORY
AT SMITH COLLEGE**
College Lane
Northampton. MA
www.smith.edu/garden
413-585-2740

**THE ORANGERIE AT
TOWER HILL BOTANIC GARDEN**
11 French Drive
Boylston, MA
www.towerhillbg.org
508-869-6111

ROGER CLAPP GREENHOUSES
University of Maine
College Avenue
Orono, ME
www.umaine.edu/mafes/
farms/littlefield.htm
207-581-3112

**CHARLES H. SMITH
GREENHOUSE**
at Roger Williams Park, 1000
Elmwood Ave., Providence, RI
www.rogerwilliamsparkzoo.org/
visit/ParkGreenhouses.cfm
401-785-9450

**LOGEE'S GREENHOUSES
LTD.**
141 North Street
Danielson, CT
www.logees.com
888-330-8038

ELIZABETH PARK
Postpect and
Asylum Avenues
Hartfort, CT
www.elizabethpark.com
860-231-9443

There are as many types and models of greenhouses as there are cars and computers, so if you long for a leafy winter nook, do some homework before you buy.

Begin by checking with your local municipal government about building and zoning permits. Except for set-back requirements, greenhouse structures are covered by municipal bylaws only if they are permanent.

Most New Englanders prefer greenhouses attached to their homes, though free-standing ones cause fewer zoning hassles, since many communities classify them as backyard sheds. They also allow you to pick a spot with the best light. Still, try to erect it close to the house for convenience and proximity to amenities such as running water.

To provide maximum light, a greenhouse should run east to west with its longer side facing within 25 degrees of solar south. To find solar south, which is different from magnetic south, put a stick in the ground and watch during the day to see where the shadow is shortest. Solar south is the opposite direction from that shadow.

A square and level foundation is critical, especially if you're using glass. One of the cheapest, easiest options is to bolt a kit to a foundation of 4-by-4 timbers and grow plants in the dirt floor or on raised earthen beds. A high, dry location ensures adequate drainage.

Ventilation is also key, as temperatures can get surprisingly hot on sunny days. Many people install an electric, thermostatically controlled exhaust fan high in one wall and intake air vents low on the opposite wall to drain hot air. Others use solar-powered vent openers. Larger greenhouses experience less daily temperature fluctuation than small ones.

Jones used to heat the greenhouse he built with a kit some 40 years ago, but when fuel oil prices shot up, he went solar. Not only did he save money, but whiteflies, mealy bugs and aphids disappeared with the drop in temperature. A large tub of water that retains heat, plus heat that leaks through the walls of the house, keep the lean-to greenhouse above freezing all winter.

He added a second greenhouse as a "vestibule" to solve the problem of a front door that used to open directly into the living room. Now, guests pass blooming camellias upon entering his home.

The third greenhouse is a large, free-standing, solar structure of translucent fiberglass connected to the main house through an underground passage. "Doing all the work myself, I spent less than a thousand dollars on each of them," he says. "Because they're solar, they don't cost money to run. If anything, there's a net gain because they help insulate the house."

Of course, there are alternatives to greenhouses for those who want more winter gardening space. Consider converting an open porch into a growing space by insulating the ceiling and floor and covering the openings with polycarbonate panels. Also, grow lights can give seedlings a head start in the basement.

Just remember, a greenhouse full of plants is like a pet: Someone has to care for it. So think twice if your current solution to the winter blahs is extended visits to Florida.

On the other hand, there's no end to the expensive gadgets you can add to a greenhouse. There's also even an invention called a "Sensaphone" that will monitor your greenhouse temperature and humidity while you're away and call you with a voice synthesizer if anything goes wrong. Then you call your neighbor.

WHERE TO BUY

CHARLEY'S GREENHOUSE & GARDEN SUPPLIES
17979 State Route 536
Mount Vernon, WA 98273
www.charleysgreenhouse.com
800-322-4707

GARDENER'S SUPPLY
128 Intervale Road
Burlington, VT 05401
www.gardeners.com
888-833-1412

GARDENSTYLES
2385 Goodhue Street
Red Wing, MN 55066
www.gardenstyles.com
800-356-8890

GLASS STRUCTURES LIMITED
296 Irving Street
Framingham, MA 01705
www.glassstructures.com
508-877-6457

JANCO GREENHOUSES
9390 Davis Avenue
Laurel, MD 20723
www.jancoinc.com
800-323-6933

ORLANDO GREENHOUSE SALES INC.
35A Warren Street
Westborough, MA 01581
www.orlandogreenhouse.com
508-335-6257

SUNGLOW SOLAR GREENHOUSES
214 21 Street
Southeast Auburn, WA 98032
800-647-0606

TURNER GREENHOUSES
1500 Highway 117
South Goldsboro, NC 27530
www.turnergreenhouses.com
800-672-4770

Above: This Cattleya orchid doesn't mind if you call it a hothouse flower. (Boston Globe photo/ Pat Greenhouse)

Above: If global warming continues, one day even drilling won't get syrup from New England's sugar maple trees. (Boston Globe photo/ Bill Greene)

TOO WARM FOR SYRUP?

GARDENERS KEEP A KEEN EYE ON THE WEATHER, so we're more aware than our neighbors that global warming appears to be already here.

Since 1990, the United States has had its 10 warmest years on record, according to the National Academy of Science. We experience this personally with favorite plants such as our lilacs, which are blooming six to 12 days earlier than in past decades, and we see it in New England's longer growing season (between the last spring frost and the first fall frost), which is eight days longer on average today than in 1950, according to the Climate Change Research Center at the University of New Hampshire in Durham.

If you feel like planting camellia, banana or fig trees in New England, go for it. Some years, they're making it through the winter. On the other hand, so is kudzu, the plant that ate the South.

In the long run, changes in weather, air quality, and weed and pest activity due to global warming will challenge our food production, our natural environment and perhaps eventually, some warn, our civilization.

Still, a longer growing season and warmer winters sounds attractive. Can global warming be a guilty pleasure that is good for gardening, at least in the short term (which means our lifetimes)?

"It depends on whether you see the glass as half empty or half full," says Richard Bisgrove, co-author of a recent study on global warming and gardening. It was commissioned by the UK Climate Impacts Programme in England and sponsored by the Royal Horticultural Society and the National Trust, with the support of Prince Charles, a keen gardener.

Bisgrove and his colleague, professor Paul Hadley at the University of Reading, applied the United Kingdom's climate change computer scenarios to gardening issues. They plugged in both a "low emissions" scenario, dependent on the use of clean and efficient technologies, and a "high emissions" scenario based on rapid international economic growth and a reliance on fossil fuels.

Bisgrove's more aggressive model predicts that by 2080, the south of England will enjoy a Mediterranean climate with a year-round growing season.

"Sir Francis Bacon wrote that the English climate is great for being outdoors, but not for standing still. That's why we all garden," he quips. "Maybe we'll turn into a culture where we sit around in the shade sipping margaritas."

Of course, there's more to global warming than rising temperatures, and Bisgrove also looked at the effects of rising carbon dioxide levels on weather patterns.

Left: When there's no skiing at Gunstock in the middle of winter, a New Hampshire resident might just as well get out his metal detector and go looking for other sources of income. (Boston Globe photo/ Wendy Maeda)

Noxious weeds... already eat up 2,300 acres a day and cost $13 billion a year.

Left and below: Sap buckets and a tap will take whatever the maple trees have to give. (Boston Globe photos/ Bill Greene)

Plants love carbon dioxide, which they use in photosynthesis. If carbon dioxide levels double, as widely predicted, plant growth will increase by as much as 50 percent, according to Bisgrove's report. The resulting super plants will be sturdier, larger and also perhaps less appetizing to chewing insects. Some plants also may need less watering and fertilizing (because, to get technical, a reduction in the numbers and opening of stomatal pores on leaf surfaces will slow water loss). That sounds good, but the high-fiber content also will make once-succulent veggies such as beans and asparagus less appetizing to humans. And wait till you see the weeds!

Noxious weeds, mostly introduced from abroad, already eat up 2,300 acres a day and cost $13 billion a year in this country. L.H. Ziska, plant physiologist at the USDA's lab in Beltsville, MD, says the chief beneficiaries of this carbon dioxide bonanza will be weeds with big, deep roots such as Canada thistle. Ragweed, quackgrass and, yes, kudzu also seem to particularly thrive on high carbon dioxide levels. This is why weeds really are more tenacious in cities, where carbon dioxide levels are already high.

Ziska's experiments also found that the efficacy of modern weed killers decreases when carbon dioxide levels are high.

Bisgrove's British study predicts decreases in spring, summer and autumn rains.

"Winter rainfall will be increasingly concentrated in heavy downpours," he predicts, resulting in flooding and run-off rather than recharging of aquifers, and widespread water shortages. "That's partly because a warmer atmosphere holds more water. Flood plains will become critically important and tidal surges will increase along the coasts." We've already seen this in New Orleans, which lost much of its productive flood plain because of development.

What about New England? Fluctuations in the jet stream, topography, changing ocean currents and sea-surface temperatures make our weather difficult to predict.

The big horticultural losers here certainly will include cool-season vegetables and crops such as maple syrup and potatoes. Some have also predicted problems with fruit setting for temperature-sensitive plants such as peppers, beans and tomatoes.

"The biggest risks will be to perennials and trees," says John Reilly of the Joint Program on the Science and Policy of Global Change at the Massachusetts Institute of Technology. Most government studies have focused on annual crops such as grains, cotton, potatoes and sugar beets.

"Better models are essential," he says. "There's not much interest from the government. Research on the impacts of climate change is a relatively low priority. More of the focus is on energy technologies that it is hoped would reduce emissions." ❀

GARDENER'S WEEK 1

Amaryllis: Place potted bulbs near a window where they'll receive strong sunlight, then water once. Resume weekly watering when plants start to sprout. When stalks begin to lengthen, give each pot a quarter turn every couple of days to keep stalks from bending toward the light and eventually tumbling over when they produce their large heavy flowers.

Birds: Providing fresh water is as important as filling your bird feeders each evening. An outdoor water heating unit can keep birdbaths from freezing.

Christmas greens: When you're done with them, spread these around the perennial garden as mulch to help keep the ground frozen during premature February thaws that could damage dormant plant roots. This is also a good time to prune evergreens and use the prunings as winter mulch. Cut branches should keep their needles all winter.

Christmas trees: Congratulations if yours lasted through New Year's Day. Now get rid of it, immediately. As previously advised, remove all decorations, lights, tinsel and any nails used in the base of the trunk before recycling. You also can cut up the tree for valuable winter garden mulch, or leave it whole and set it outdoors next to the bird feeders to provide cover for nervous but hungry birds. Just don't try to burn the tree as firewood or it may contribute to a creosote build-up in your chimney.

Houseplants: Give them a lukewarm shower to remove dust. Use a humidifier to discourage red spider mites by raising humidity around plants. Spray plants with a mister and fertilize lightly.

Orchids: Don't allow water to collect inside flowers when watering or it will shorten their duration.

Snowstorm damage: Late winter storms often produce heavy, wet snow. To help prevent damage, gently brush snow from evergreen trees and shrubs before it freezes. Prune any damaged branches, or hire a professional certified arborist to do larger jobs that require tree climbing.

Whitefly: Put yellow sticky traps above the foliage of affected houseplants and brush the leaves regularly to disturb the tiny pests. You can also try sucking them up with a vacuum cleaner. A more conventional treatment would be spraying tops and undersides with insecticidal soap.

Above photos, left to right:

Christmas tree recycled as mulch

Merserve holly

Polka dot plant

Orchid

Amaryllis

Elephant ears

(Boston Globe photos/ Jonathan Wiggs, Bill Greene; holly, polka dot plant and elephant ears photos courtesy of www. parkseed.com)

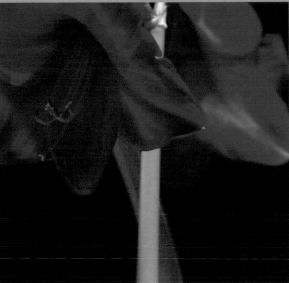

GARDENER'S WEEK 2

Birds: Dead and dying trees are magnets for birds, notably woodpeckers, who like to excavate nesting holes later used by other birds. Even if you have to remove dead limbs for safety, leave the trunk if at all possible and you will soon have a vertical bird condominium.

Evergreens: Tie up branches that have been splayed by snow.

Lawns: Avoid walking on wet lawns or on frozen grass unless there's a covering of snow, because you could compress the soil and in the spring see your footprints as if they were set in wet cement.

Red spider mites: These common houseplant pests thrive in dry conditions and will usually disappear if the infected plants are sprayed or misted with cold water. Increasing humidity with a humidifier will help keep the mites from returning, as well as reduce other problems such as yellowing leaves, browning edges, or leaf drop that forced-air heating can create.

Spring thaw: A general warming trend known as the January thaw often occurs about this time. Unfortunately this is only temporary, but when it comes, watch for flights of bees and listen for spring peepers. Replenish mulch on exposed areas to help keep the ground safely frozen until true spring. Check plants such as coral bells for roots that have been heaved out of the soil by fluctuating temperatures, and cover them with dirt and mulch.

Squirrels: If they're hogging your bird feeder, try using thistle seeds, which attract finches but are not favored by squirrels.

Trees: When cutting wood from fallen branches with a chainsaw, use protective goggles and wear a thick jacket, but no loose clothing. Don't insert the chain into a previous cut or use it on wet wood or raise the saw above your waist.

TOP 10

Trees and shrubs tolerant of road salt for street-side planting:

10 **Blue spruce**

9 **Catalpa**

8 **Eastern arborvitae**

7 **Honey locust**

6 **Horse chestnut**

5 **Juniper**

4 **Mugo pine**

3 **Sycamore**

2 **Sumac**

1 **Rosa rugosa**

GARDENER'S WEEK 3

Houseplants: Indoor air pollution from household chemicals is higher in winter when houses are sealed up tight, but houseplants help purify the air. The best common types for helping remove benzene, ammonia, and other toxic chemicals include peace lilies and philodendrons.

Indoor lighting: Lack of good light is the most common limiting factor for growing plants indoors. Temporarily relocate shade-loving houseplants to a sunnier spot to compensate for low winter light levels. Unobstructed south- or west-facing windows will grow the greatest variety of indoor plants. However, a nearby building or other factors can affect your window light. If your hand held next to your houseplants casts a shadow with sharp edges, they are getting bright light. A hazier shadow designates medium light, and an absence of shadow means low light. Full-spectrum fluorescent lights provide good artificial light for plants and also pleasing illumination in the home.

Seed catalogs: Planning a garden and leafing through seed catalogs is educational and makes winter seem shorter. If you grow seeds indoors, winter is shorter still. Many of the best seed companies have excellent Web pages with more photos and information than can fit in a catalog. Some are designed so you can fill in the blanks to call up a personalized list of plants that fit your growing conditions, with height and color requirements to help you choose – even if you eventually send your order through the mail. Helpful sites include W. Atlee Burpee & Co. at www.burpee.com, the Park Seed Company at www.parkseed.com, Territorial Seed Company at www.territorialseed.com and Thompson & Morgan Inc. at www.thompson-morgan.com.

Shrubs: Cut branches of pussy willow, forsythia, witch hazel, cornelian dogwood and flowering quince on a seasonably warm day to force in indoor vases.

Vegetables: Seed cress into a shallow container filled with peat moss and set it in a sunny window.

KNOW YOUR TERMS

CLIMACTIC ZONE: The Department of Agriculture divides the country into numbered climactic zones based on winter temperatures. The warmest parts of southern New England are in USDA Zone 7 and the coldest parts of northern New England are in Zone 3. A plant labeled for "Zone 6" should be able to survive winters in Boston.

FORCING: Using indoor warmth to induce a cut stem or an entire plant to bloom ahead of schedule.

HALF-HARDY ANNUAL: An annual plant that tolerates light frosts.

HARDY ANNUAL: A frost-resistant annual plant that can be sown outdoors very early in spring, but will still only live one year.

HARDY: A plant that can survive winters outdoors where you live.

HARDSCAPE: Permanent landscape structures, particularly paving.

CHIPPER/SHREDDER: A machine that grinds or splinters dry leaves or woody twigs into small pieces that can be used as garden

LEAF MOLD: Partially decomposed leaves that form a rich, weed-free natural mulch and fertilizer in woodlands.

GARDENER'S WEEK 4

Birds: Keep bird feeders full and hang suet for chickadees and woodpeckers. To attract colorful blue jays and wild turkeys (both of which are making a comeback) scatter cracked corn on the ground some distance from your birdfeeder. This will also draw squirrels away from the feeder and is much less expensive than birdseed.

Camellias: They won't bloom unless they're given a rest period at 50 degrees or cooler. The same is true for acacia and winter-blooming jasmine, so if these plants fail to set buds for you, move them to a cooler spot. You can visit outstanding collections of flowering camellias in the 1820 camellia house at the Lyman Estate in Waltham, MA, and Tower Hill Botanic Garden Orangerie in Boylston, MA.

Hardiness zones: When placing mail orders for hardy plants, keep in mind that each variety has a zonal designation indicating how far north it can survive over future winters. Buy plants marked USDA Zone 6 or lower if you live in Eastern Massachusetts or along the North Shore. Cape Cod and the Islands and southern Rhode Island are in Zone 7. Most of Central and Western Massachusetts New Hampshire, Maine and Vermont are in Zone 5. Mountainous areas and the far north are in Zone 4. You can try growing plants that are supposed to be too tender for your zone by planting them on the south side of a house or in spots with good drainage that are sheltered from wind. Mulching heavily and improving soil drainage also help marginally hardy plants survive the winter.

Winter moths: If your trees suffered from inchworms last May and you noticed swarms of moths attracted to lights last winter, contract to have your trees sprayed in April. Arborists will be very busy then, so reserve them now. The larvae of winter moths (Operophtera brumata) are small green inchworms that feed on buds and leaves of trees and shrubbery in the early spring. The young caterpillars tunnel into buds of oak, maple, linden, elm, apple, crabapple, cherry, blueberry and certain spruces. Eggs can hatch as soon as late March or as late as late April. Winter moths are best controlled using a biological pesticide known as Spinosad, produced by a microbe. It's safe around people, pets and wildlife. Do two applications at 7- to 14-day intervals beginning at bud break. Homeowners desiring greatest control should also schedule a dormant oil treatment to smother egg masses.

Above photos, left to right:

Greenhouse orchids

Bluejay

Chickadee at a Droll Yankee feeder

Dwarf Alberta spruce

(Boston Globe photos/ Wendy Maeda, Mark Wilson, Pat Greenhouse, Tom Herde)

Moth orchid (Phalaenopsis).

These most reliable of orchids can make any room look swank. Though available in colors, the white ones (pictured here is a 'Harlequin') have the most and largest flowers, and really do look like hovering moths. They like east- or west-facing windows, a nearby humidifier and warmth. (Boston Globe photo/ Jonathan Wiggs)

Lady slipper orchids (Paphiopedilum) are also easy.
(Boston Globe photo/ Jonathan Wiggs)

FEBRUARY

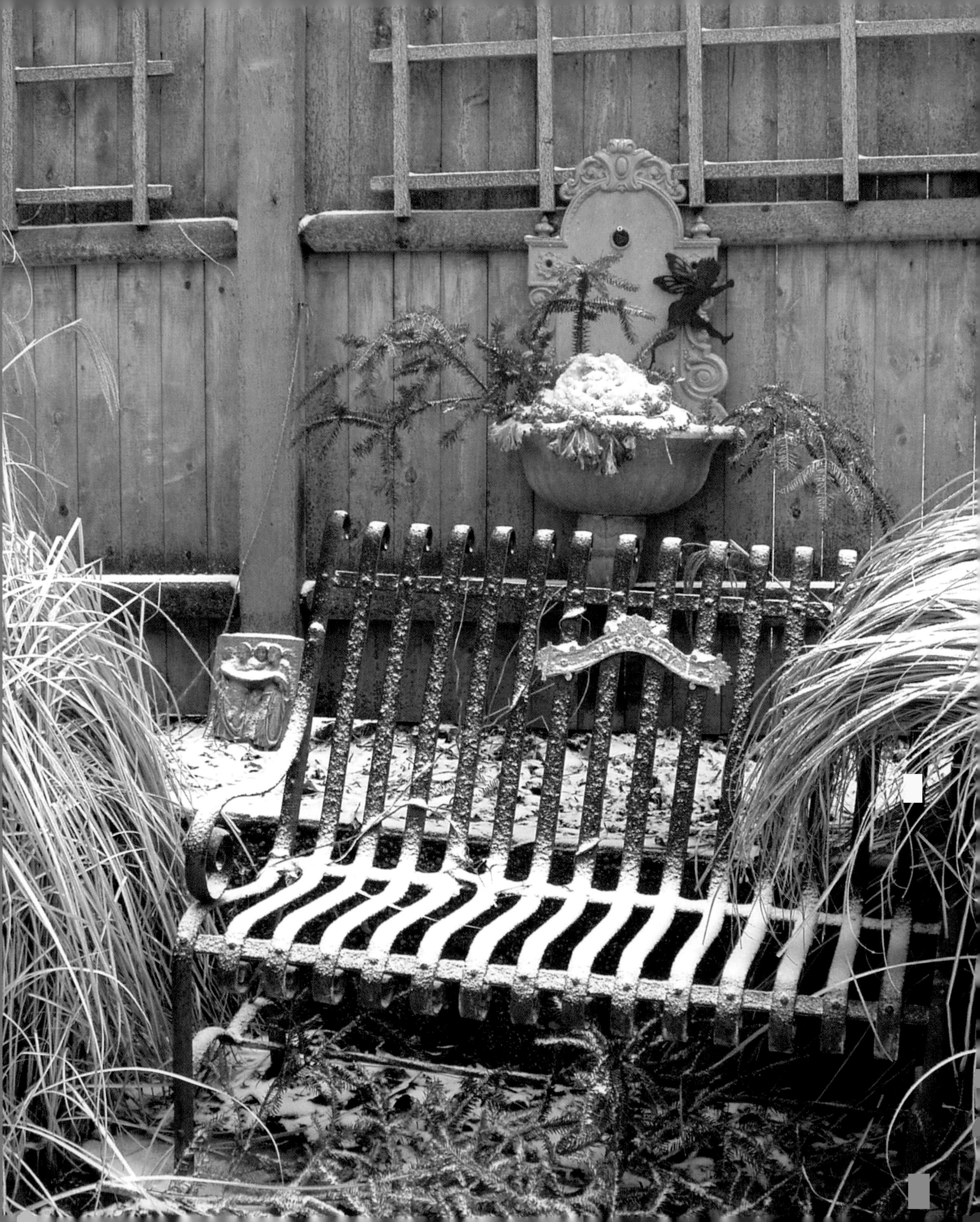

WINTER GARDENS (SERIOUSLY)

IS "WINTER GARDEN" AN OXYMORON?

Certainly, few American gardens are designed to look good during our longest season. The typical outstanding feature in my own landscape is the Christmas lights I haven't taken down yet. Most Americans resent winter, and ignore their gardens then. As a result, their winter view is often the brown scars of dormant perennial beds.

It doesn't have to be like that. The right plants and garden architecture can supply an artful winter tableau. So says Sydney Eddison, who loves this season and wrote a fine book about winter gardening a decade ago called "The Unsung Season: Gardens and Gardeners in Winter" (Houghton Mifflin), which went largely unread.

Now in her seventies, Eddison believes it can take a lifetime of gardening to appreciate the winter landscape. "The older you get, the better you like it," she says. "You can rest. It's not a demanding season physically, which in itself is wonderful. There's something very calming about the black and white colors, the stripped-down aspect. As you get older, simplicity becomes something you strive for. You'll see a cardinal and it will be a blinding spark of red light. In the summer, we take him for granted because he's competing with the flowers and all these other distractions."

Left: Create sculptural interest with a metal lawn chair, winter-beaten miscanthus ornamental grass, ornamental cabbage (in planter) and sprigs of evergreen. (Photo by Janice Page)

Creating a garden that's attractive in winter is challenging, however, even for professionals. When Ken Twombly planted his famous 3/4-acre display garden at Twombly Nurseries in Monroe, CT a decade ago, "I started with plants of winter interest because that is the hardest season," he says. "Spring, summer and fall are no-brainers."

The master plan for Tower Hill Botanic Garden in Boylston, MA, also was designed with winter in mind first, says director John Trexler: "You have to think long and hard so you have something pretty to look at for those six months."

When designing a new garden, it makes sense to plan for winter first and then work backward, agrees Eddison, because a successful winter garden depends on the structure it gets from hardscaping, architecture and mature trees and shrubs. A winter garden takes much longer to create than a spring garden, whose glory is fast-growing bulbs and perennials. "But gardeners fall in love with flowers, and that's what gets them gardening," sighs Eddison. "And then when you're too old to plant a tree and live to see it mature, that's when you get all excited about trees! We should start by planning for winter, but we don't."

Eddison, whose more recent books include "The Gardener's Palette" (McGraw-Hill) and "Gardens to Go: Creating and Designing a Container Garden" (Bulfinch), started winterizing her Newtown, CT, garden when she quit teaching to stay home and write in 1975. "I had time to look out my window all winter, and I thought I'd like to see something," she says. "That was the beginning of my love affair with ornamental grasses such as miscanthus and pennisetum, which looks wonderful all the time. Then I began to think about what plants I could leave standing that wouldn't have messy leaves, such as sedum 'Autumn Joy' and calamint. Far more by good luck than design, I started sticking in some evergreens, which gave me a good framework. But I have a good eye and when I saw that I had done something right, I kept at it."

The centerpiece of her garden in winter is an island bed of shrubs with contrasting shapes and colors in the middle of a long panel of flat lawn. There's a low mound of golden chamaecyparis, a tall cone of dwarf Alberta spruce, "which, after [almost 40] years, has reached 15 feet so it's not so dwarf," and a low mat of blue juniper "to nail it all to the ground." A large hollow earthenware ball glazed sky blue by an artist friend adds to the colors and geometric shapes.

Like the winter cardinal, every bit of color and form gains power in the stark winter landscape, so architectural elements such as a column, a fence, a cement urn or even lawn furniture left outside by accident assume more visual dignity than during summer. A major feature in Eddison's garden in winter is a custom-built birdbath placed 5 inches from the sliding glass doors of the breakfast room. It's heated with "one of the things you buy to keep a horse's trough thawed. The cord runs down the hollow base of the birdbath. It is one of our greatest joys to watch the birds enjoy water they don't have to work for." ❀

Left: A witch hazel prepares to bloom next to a metal bird bath. (Photo by Janice Page)

FLOWERS? NOW? IT'S WITCHCRAFT

IF YOU SUFFER FROM CABIN FEVER EACH WINTER, PLANT A WITCH HAZEL this spring. You'll probably have the first one in your neighborhood.

Most people will think it's forsythia, but witch hazel's bright-yellow flowers appear almost two months earlier, and will bloom on sunny days when temperatures are in the high 20s. (They must contain some sort of natural anti-freeze!) On cloudy days, the narrow 3/4-inch-long petals furl up. They'll curl and uncurl like party noise makers for up to six weeks, making them among the longest-blooming shrubs.

Why aren't these amazing plants on every street corner, as forsythia is? I think it's because witch hazel blooms too early. They've finished by the time the garden centers open for business in April, which is just when those too-common forsythias are flaunting themselves at the impulse buyers.

Also, unlike Europeans who are the main breeders of new witch hazels, Americans just don't think about beautifying their gardens during winter.

My first attempt at growing witch hazel started off badly because I had an old-fashioned cultivar (Hamamelis mollis 'Brevipetala') that adamantly refused to drop its old leaves. So there I would be in February, freezing, while I pulled the sorry brown things off by hand because they were completely hiding the yellow flowers. I was just about to pull out the entire shrub when I brought some cut branches indoors. The sweet smell of the flowers in the warmth of the house was unbelievable. I was hooked. I didn't care how the ugly thing looked, just as long as it smelled good. It was nothing short of a miracle to me to have flowers from my garden with that scent in February.

Most modern witch hazel varieties drop their leaves willingly, but are not as fragrant as my 'Brevipetala.' My quest has been to find the most fragrant of these better-behaved varieties.

KINDS TO CONSIDER

'PALLIDA.' Ken Twombly of Twombly's Nursery in Connecticut points to this widely available winner of many horticultural awards. It blooms heavily with refined but very bright pale-lemon flowers with hints of chartreuse. Michael Arnum of Tower Hill Botanic Garden in Boylston, MA, served on the committee that gave Pallida the Cary Award, a kind of local plant Oscar for good performers. He agrees it's "the most fragrant of the bunch. But it will hang onto its old leaves." 'Pallida' is wider spreading than vase-shaped butter-yellow 'Arnold's Promise,' which also has a nice fragrance, though not as strong. 'Arnold's Promise' is a proper Bostonian that always drops its old leaves.

'ANGELLY' AND 'BARNSTEDT GOLD.' The country's leading expert on witch hazel, Tim Brotzman, sells 40 varieties in his Ohio wholesale nursery and grows more than 80 types in his garden. He evaluates all the new European hybrids.

"Every year, we plant three or four new ones," he says. The two favorites with his visitors are sweet-smelling, heavy-blooming 'Angelly,' a yellow Dutch hybrid with much bigger flowers than 'Arnold's Promise,' and 'Barnstedt Gold,' a German golden yellow with flowers that are even bigger and earlier, but not as powerfully fragrant.

Witch hazel flowers look like tassels the size of a quarter and can be orange, ruby, gold and lemon. Fall foliage is usually yellow, though some have red and orange autumn leaves. 'Hiltingbury' has the best fall foliage, Brotzman says.

All witch hazels have some scent, but most of the notably sweet-smelling ones are yellow bloomers. Brotzman thinks 'Orange Beauty,' an overlooked older variety, is perhaps the most fragrant orange flowering one. The most common red variety, 'Diane,' and the most common orange, 'Jelana,' both sometimes hold onto their leaves and have mild scents, Twombly says.

ASIAN WITCH HAZELS. These reached Western gardens about a century ago. Unlike their American woodland cousins, which bloom in November and December, Asian witch hazels flower February to April. They make better garden plants because of their larger flowers and sweeter scent. Most powerfully fragrant are the early-blooming yellow Chinese witch hazels (Hamamelis mollis), such as my 'Brevipetala.' Perhaps there's a genetic link between powerful scent and ugly leaf retention. The Japanese witch hazel (H. japonica) blooms a little later, drops its old leaves nicely, and can have reddish flowers and leaves that can turn shades of red and orange in the fall - but it is less fragrant. Most garden witch hazels are crosses between these two Asian species. Generally speaking, the more Chinese mollis genes in the mix, the more fragrance; the more japonica genes, the redder the flowers and fall foliage.

CULTIVATING WITCHES

Witch hazels are easy to grow and largely pest-free, though deer will browse them lightly. They start blooming young, and even mail-order plants may bloom within 12 months. They tolerate a lot of shade, and you can site them under a canopy of trees, as I did, though they will produce more flowers in full sun. Hardy through all but the coldest parts of New England, witch hazels like acid soil, which makes them good companions for broad-leaved, shade-tolerant evergreens such as rhododendrons, mountain laurels and andromeda.

I think the biggest drawback is that all witch hazels grow large, and, even worse, they grow wide. They start out as shrubs, but over a couple of decades grow into multi-stemmed trees about 15 feet tall and wide. That's more space than many gardeners want to devote to a winter plant. Also, they aren't drought tolerant. They need good drainage and will drown in a low spot. Heavy clay soil should be amended with leaf mold, peat moss or compost when you plant them, and mulching is important.

Incidentally, the name comes from colonists who discovered native North American witch hazel blooming wild in the woods in December and attributed magical properties to it, using the twigs for water divining. I tend to agree that any plant that blooms in December, or February, has a bit of voodoo. ❀

Above: Hamamelis virginiana, our native wild witch hazel, in bloom. (Photo courtesy of New England Wild Flower Society/ William Cullina)

GARDENER'S WEEK 1

African violets: These houseplants will bloom year-round. If yours aren't, they may need some adjustments. Long, upward-pointed leafstalks tell you the light is too weak; yellow-reddish leaves and hanging leafstalks mean light is too strong. Unobstructed east or west windows have the right amount of light. Don't let the soil dry out between waterings and use a weak dose of fertilizer weekly.

Azaleas: Those sold as flowering houseplants and as holiday gifts aren't hardy, but you can keep them alive to rebloom 16 months from now if you can provide four hours of indirect sunlight, such as from an east window. Daytime temperatures should be no higher than 65 degrees, and 10 degrees less at night. New growth will be leggy if conditions are too warm. Put the plant in your sink and give it a weekly shower to prevent spider mites. Old leaves drop normally but if new ones drop, the plant needs more light or water. Fertilize with acid fertilizer in April and July and when repotting. Let it spend the summer outdoors in a shady, protected spot but keep it constantly moist.

Compost: Kitchen waste such as vegetable and fruit trimmings, cut flowers and coffee grounds can be collected in a bin under the sink and added periodically to the compost pile. Avoid composting meat, fish, dairy products, fats or grease, which will attract animals.

Gardening websites: Find clubs, post questions and swap seeds and books in six languages at www.gardenweb.com. Swap seeds also at www.seedswappers.com. There are links to many garden subjects and international horticultural organizations at www.gardenscape.com.

Herbs: Particularly informative mail-order catalogs and websites for herb-lovers include the following:

RICHTERS, 357 Highway 47, Goodwood, Ontario, L0C 1A0, Canada (www.richters.com; 905-640-6677).

JOHNNY'S SELECTED SEEDS, 955 Benton Ave., Winslow, ME 04901 (www.johnnyseeds.com; 877-564-6697).

WELL-SWEEP HERB FARM, 205 Mt. Bethel Road, Port Murray, NJ 07865 (www.wellsweep.com; 908-852-5390).

TERRITORIAL SEED COMPANY, P.O. Box 158, Cottage Grove, OR 97424 (www.territorialseed.com; 800-626-0866).

NICHOL'S GARDEN NURSERY, 1190 Old Salem Road NE, Albany, OR 97321 (www.gardennursery.com; 800-422-3985).

HERB SOCIETY OF AMERICA, The New England Unit of the has an informational website at www.neuhsa.homestead.com.

Orchids: The easiest orchids to grow are paphiopedilum (lady slippers) and phalaenopsis (moth orchids). Both prefer an east window or a southern exposure with shading, perhaps by a lace curtain. They like low light levels. If you hold your hand with spread fingers above a plant on a sunny day, its shadow should look like an indistinct mitten. A sharp shadow with all fingers clearly visible means the area has too much light for these orchids.

Paperwhites: If you're growing these fragrant narcissi in pebbles, keep the water level at the bottom of the bulbs. Discard the plants after blooming.

Rhododendrons: It's normal for these shrubs to curl their leaves like cigars and droop in very cold weather.

GARDENER'S WEEK 2

Birds: Chickadees, titmice, starlings and purple finches often begin their spring songs this week.

Botanical Latin: It's good to learn the Latin names for plants because common names for the same plant often vary from one place to another, and many plants don't have common names at all. Most garden plants have two parts to their Latin name. The first is the genus, which designates a group of plants and is capitalized. The second is the species, usually in the form of an adjective, such as repens (creeping) or albus (white) or sempervirens (evergreen) that describes some aspect of the plant. The species isn't capitalized. The abbreviation "v." or "var." refers to the variety, and distinguishes plants of the same species with some different characteristics. "Cv." stands for cultivated variety. Cultivars names are capitalized and enclosed in single quotes.

Catalogs: It's time to start placing orders. Make sure to keep records of your transactions so you know what's coming for planning purposes. Team up with a neighbor or friend to buy seeds, since each packet yields much more than one person needs.

Cyclamen: They like bright indirect light and cool temperatures.

Houseplants: At night during extremely cold weather, tender plants on a windowsill can be damaged if they're behind closed curtains. Cyclamen and begonias can take cooler nighttime temperatures than other flowering plants. Most other species prefer temperatures no lower than 60 degrees.

Orchids: Don't allow the roots of paphiopedilums, the orchids that look like lady's slippers, to dry out.

Valentine's Day: To extend the life of a bouquet of roses, fill a vase with hot water and add a couple of drops of bleach. Cut a quarter-inch off the end of each rose stem under running water with sharp shears, then store the roses in the vase overnight in the coolest, darkest spot in the house. Next day, empty the vase and refill it with hot (but not scalding) water. You can add a teaspoon of vinegar to keep bacteria from growing or three-quarters of a teaspoon of floral preservative or sugar. Then recut the rose stems again under water and arrange them.

Wildlife: Something is browsing your garden, but what? Deer have no upper teeth and leave ragged edges on twig ends and evergreens, while rabbits leave sharp clipped ends on vegetation. Deer also are taller, of course.

Winterscaping: If your winter landscape looks barren, make a note to plant some evergreens this spring. This is a good time to consider the hardscaping, or "bones," of your garden for future placement of stonework, fencing, trees, outdoor sculpture and other year-round features.

Above photos, left to right:

African Violets

Wild turkey

Winter evergreens

Miscanthus

Paperwhites

(African violets and evergreens photos courtesy of www.parkseed. com; miscanthus and paperwhites photos by Janice Page; Boston Globe photo of turkey/ Tom Landers)

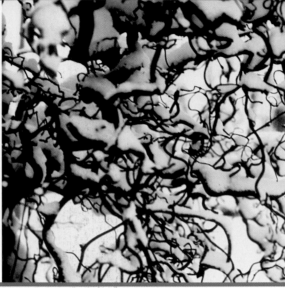
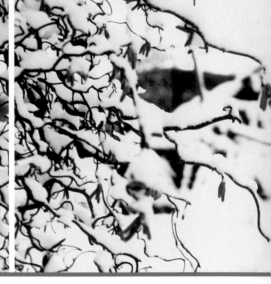

GARDENER'S WEEK 3

Amaryllis: After blooming is finished, you can attempt a repeat performance next year by cutting off the faded flowers but leaving the stalks and letting the foliage emerge. Keep watering and fertilizing until June, then move the pots outdoors into partial shade. In early August, turn the pots on their sides so that dryness will induce dormancy. When night temperatures dip into the 50s, bring the potted bulbs inside and store them in a dark place for two months before reintroducing light and water. (Then cross your fingers; it doesn't always work.)

Forcing branches: Cut branches of pussy willows, cornelian dogwood (which has small yellow flowers), cherries, witch hazel or forsythia on a day when the temperature is above freezing. Recut the stems under warm water and let the branches soak overnight. Then put them in a vase of hot but not scalding water and leave them in a cool but not cold garage until the first buds begin to show color. Then display them. Change the water weekly.

Garden journals: This is a good time to start one to keep track of plans and purchases, and, later, what's blooming when.

Houseplants: Many prefer a slightly cooler resting period at night, so turn down the thermostat to 55 to 60 degrees when you go to bed and most of your houseplants will be happier. However, African violets and begonias may go dormant if temperatures fall below 65. Most indoor plants, especially orchids, will benefit from a small fan to help circulate air.

Kitchen scraps: How to recycle them when it's too cold to walk to the compost pile? Keep an old blender under the sink to fill with tea bags, eggshells and vegetable scraps. The rubber seal prevents odors. When full, add water, blend and pour onto your outside compost pile. The pulverizing speeds the composting process.

Seeds: You can start most perennial seeds now. Annual flower seeds that you can also plant indoors now include snapdragons, begonias, pansies, dusty miller and browallia. Use seed-growing trays under a light source that will provide steady temperatures of about 80 degrees to aid germination. Bottom heat is even better. You can place seedling trays over (but never on) radiators, or buy an electric "grow mat." Cover the trays of dampened soil mix with plastic wrap and add very little or no additional water until the first true leaves sprout. Hang height-adjustable fluorescent grow lights 6 inches above seedlings and run them 14-18 hours per day. Raise the lights as seedlings grow taller.

Tender bulbs: Check stored dahlia tubers and spray them with mist to prevent shriveling, but don't spray gladiola corms, which need to remain dry.

Wild flower seeds: The New England Wild Flower Society's highly regarded Seed and Book catalog is available in at www.newfs.org or call 508-877-7630 ext. 3601.

GARDENER'S WEEK 4

Evergreens: Reapply Wilt-Proof or another antidesiccant on a day when temperatures are above 45 degrees to help keep leaves from turning brown.

First spring blooms: Look for little white snowdrops, yellow bushes of witch hazel (which resemble sparse forsythia) and low nodding hellebores or Lenten roses, a murky green and plum-colored evergreen perennial related to buttercups (not roses).

Flowers: Start pansies indoors from seed.

Heavy equipment: If you're planning work in your yard that requires heavy equipment, such as cherry pickers for pruning or backhoes for transporting rocks, this may be the time to do it because the frozen ground means fewer ruts and less damage to your lawn.

Hemlocks: As soon as the weather warms, spray hemlocks attacked by wooly adelgids with a mix of one ounce of dormant oil for each gallon of water. Spray up under the needles, which need to be entirely covered and must dry for three hours before temperatures drop below freezing.

Houseplants: Air in houses is often dry this time of year, so pay attention to watering plants. Sometimes the soil surface is dry but the soil under the surface is wet. So feel for soil moisture by inserting your finger up to the first knuckle into the growing medium. Only water if the tip of your finger feels dry. Avoid putting houseplants near heating and ventilating ducts, fireplaces and drafts, or in any place subject to excess heat and dry air from appliances.

Orchids: Repot them annually. The best time is immediately after they have finished flowering. First water the plants, then take the orchids from their pots. Remove all potting medium from around the roots using fingers and a soft stream of water. Repot the plants in pots that fit the roots without bending them, using the same type of growing medium they were already growing in. Water repotted orchids sparingly. A wide variety of aids for growing orchids can be ordered from Kelley's Korner Orchid Supplies, P.O. Box G, Kittery, ME, 03904 (207-439-0922, www.kkorchid.com).

Pruning: This can begin after the coldest part of the winter has passed, but before growth begins. However, don't prune spring-flowering shrubs until after they bloom.

Websites: When looking through catalogs and planning what plants to buy this spring, you can find the results of comparative trials in a user-friendly format at the Chicago Botanic Garden's websites at www.chicagobotanic.org and at www.eplants.org. The garden's plant evaluation program rates commercially available plants, both old and new, that grow in USDA hardiness zones 4 to 7, which covers all of New England.

Above photos, left to right:

Greenhouse hydrangeas, zoned geraniums and coleus

'Harry Lauder's Walking Stick' (Corylus avellana 'Contorta')

Amaryllis

Aloe vera grows indoors

(Greenhouse garden photo courtesy of Netherlands Flower Bulb Information Center); 'Harry Lauder's Walking Stick' courtesy of www.parkseed.com; Aloe vera courtesy of Proven Winners® – www.provenwinners.com; Amaryllis photo courtesy of John Scheepers Flower Bulbs)

Snowdrops (Galanthus).

Even earlier than crocus, these are the very first bulbs to bloom in the garden, a down-payment on spring. Their tiny white and green pendants look like teardrops. Plant them in September by the dozens, 3 inches deep and 3 inches apart in partial shade.

(Above photo courtesy of John Scheepers Flower Bulbs; photo at left courtesy of Netherlands Flower Bulb Information Center)

AUTHOR'S NOTE

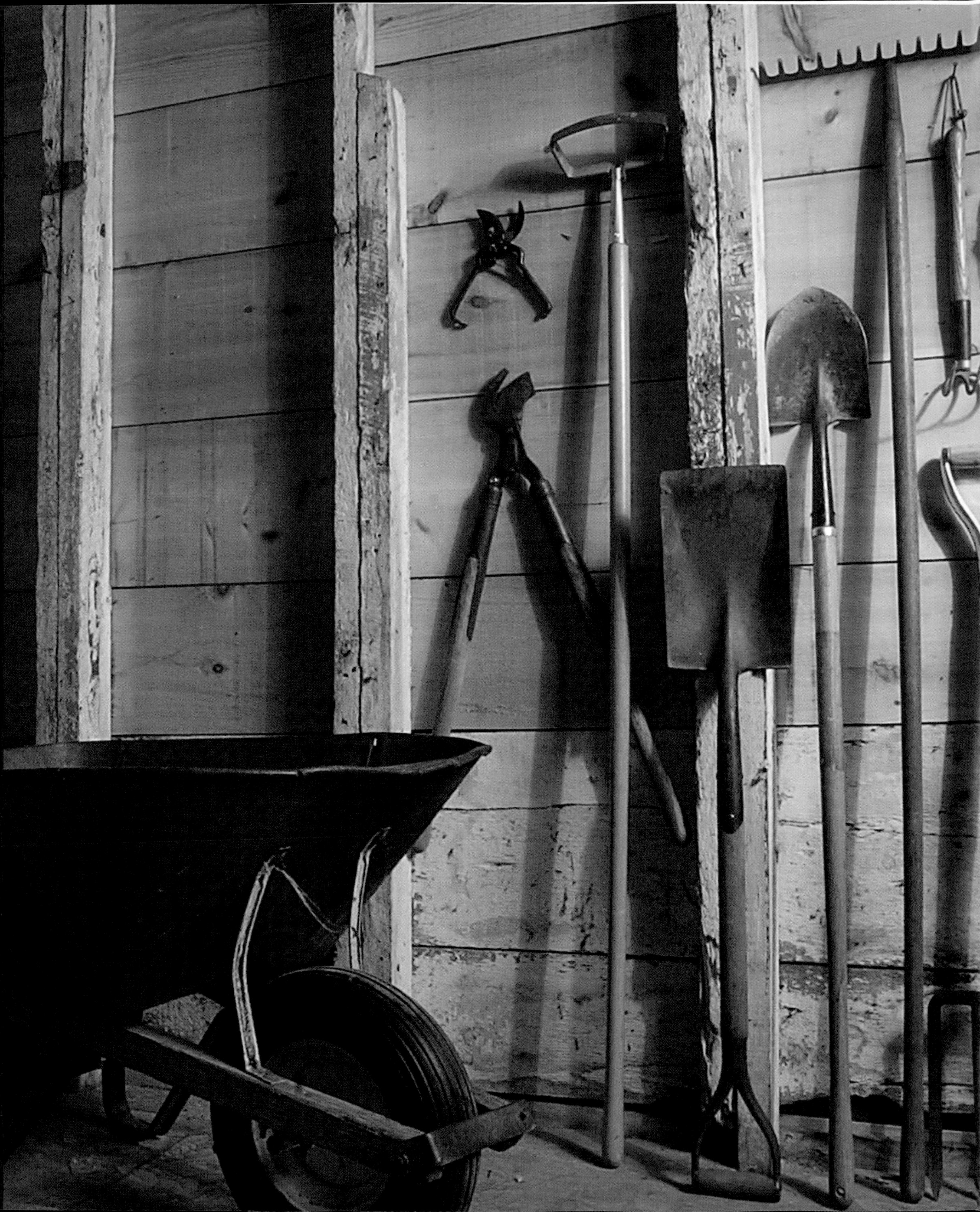

Living With Fleuromania

WINTER IS WHAT MADE ME A GARDENER.

I fell for gardening suddenly and hard some 30 ago when I lived in Detroit, where the winters are so long and dreadful thcy create a kind of annual madness. A Burpee catalog fell into my hands one January day and I was a goner. Planning a sunny, color-saturated garden was a mental escape from light deprivation, reading garden catalogs an effective antidepressant.

The painfully slow unfolding of spring became a quest to realize the paradise I had imagined over the winter. The real gardens were never as good as the imagined ones, for horticulture is not easy. But it is vast. There are always new plants and new methods to try, and the learning process became as much a source of fascination as the elusive goal of bountiful blooms and perfect vegetables.

Left: A few essential gardening tools (see Top 10 list, Page 109) hang out in Carol Stocker's antique woodshed, which once was a "summer kitchen." (Boston Globe photo/ Essdras M. Suarez)

Not atypically, I passed through a phase of total obsession, when all I wanted to talk about was gardening. I sought out others who spoke in botanical Latin and knew their stuff. They tolerated and indulged me, as I now smile warmly at new gardeners I meet who are in the throes of "fleuromania," a term coined by the Victorians who recognized it as a common affliction of their era.

My mania abated after a few years, but fortunately my interest did not. When I became the Boston Globe's gardening writer in the early 1990s I was cast in the role of an expert, which I was not. But I had access to those who were and I was able to use my true skills as a reporter and writer to find them and convey their information in prose powered by enthusiasm. And my own expertise grew with every story I researched.

I've also witnessed my readers' gardening interest and knowledge growing alongside my own. While my parents didn't garden, I belong to a generation that does. More than a century ago, the Arts & Crafts Movement developed as a reaction to industrialization. I think I've been part of a contemporary green movement with similarly large political and cultural subtexts that has developed in reaction to the mass production of food and the almost complete severing of our interaction with nature, and that this was first manifested in the creation of Earth Day in 1970.

The rebirth of gardening, after a long fallow period in the 1950s and early 1960s, started with the simple urge for living greenery in a plastic world, expressed through the rediscovery of houseplants. In a quantum leap, this was followed by a boundlessly optimistic generation's bravura attempts to actually grow their own food in the 1970s. Bay Staters led the way in all this, first with Boston Globe garden columnist Thalassa Cruso's popular books and 1966-69 WGBH-TV show "Making Things Grow," and then in 1975 by James Underwood Crockett's and Russ Morash's "The Victory Garden," also from WGBH-TV, which became a national sensation.

But growing vegetables is truly one of the most difficult types of gardening. Many more newcomers were eventually enticed by the decorative possibilities presented by a seemingly endless assortment of perennial plants that first appeared in local nurseries in the 1980s, and which were so much more inspiring than the pallid palette of annuals then for sale. Soon gardens started getting fancy, as decorative fencing, pergolas and gazebos made a comeback, followed by patios and terracing.

By the 1990s, the garden was becoming on "outdoor room" with well-designed, weatherproof furniture and creative lighting. Container gardening, dwarf evergreens, tropical plants and exotic new annuals, often with colorful foliage, also became hallmarks of the modern garden, while the study of garden history blossomed at the Landscape Institute of the Arnold Arboretum, leading to the restoration of many lost landscapes.

Above: The main perennial border in Carol Stocker's garden is defined by a split-rail cedar fence. (Boston Globe photo/ Pam Berry)

We entered the 2000s giddy about sophisticated design. Though aggressive modernism has long been apparent in commercial landscape architecture, it is finally making inroads into the private landscapes of the wealthy through the work of a generation of talented designers, many influenced by or affiliated with the Harvard Graduate School of Design. The last decade has also seen the increased use of fine art sculpture in gardens.

But the most important development I've witnessed is the mainstreaming of organic gardening and lawn care and the vastly increased use of native plants, with a significant contribution from the New England Wild Flower Society based in Framingham, MA. Whereas other developments are mostly stylistic trends, this one goes to the heart of the matter by using the garden to teach us about our relationship with the larger natural world.

Like many people, when I started gardening I had about a three-year grace period before insect pests, plant diseases and serious weeds discovered what I was up to. At that point, a war against nature typically breaks out as one tries to shield cosseted garden plants from the onslaught. This kind of thinking goes way back to Tudor knot gardens and the formality of Versailles, when gardening was viewed as imposing order on the chaos of wildness. But the advent of modern chemicals has rendered this age-old attitude easily toxic, as health-conscious people began to realize.

Most garden plants are the horticultural equivalent of domesticated animals. Like corgis, Holstein cows and Siamese fighting fish, they have little in common with their wild ancestors and could not survive on their own. By abandoning my delphiniums to their fate and inviting tough native plants such as butterfly weed into my yard, I garden more like a referee than a martinet.

Rejecting dangerous chemicals changed my incipient war on nature into a partnership. It also encouraged wild birds and butterflies to see my yard as a habitat. And I began to see it that way, too.

This expanded view of gardening has helped make me, and I think many others, more aware of the big picture. Unfortunately, that picture has become dire. Today's gardener is contending with global forces such as an international economy that has brought many foreign pests to New England in just the last 15 years, including the lily leaf beetle, the hemlock woolly adelgid and the winter moth. Hard as these are on our gardens, we know they're even more of a threat to our woodlands, as is acid rain, the pandemic of diseases attacking our weakened native trees, and the imported invasive plants that overrun millions of acres of land each year.

Most of the problems gardeners see involve environmental degradation, but global warming is an actual threat to survival. We see evidence of it in recent droughts and devistating flash floods. You don't have to live in New Orleans to agree with Bruce Babbitt, President Clinton's former secretary of the interior, when he says, "Climate change is the most dangerous, ominous environmental transformation of our time."

Working outdoors in the garden in an era when life is largely climate-controlled and sedentary guarantees us gardeners enough sunlight and sweat to strengthen our bones and unclench our minds. And spiritually speaking, a personal hands-on relationship with the earth is no small thing. But rather than being an escape, gardening has become a window on the world. It makes me and my gardening peers aware of and responsive to problems that are less visible to those who live their lives indoors. And that's what makes us a movement. ❀

Right: Carol Stocker chats with passing neighbor Margaret Farrell under her cedar pergola. **Far right:** Russian clematis 'Perestroika' and a hedge of peonies point to a nearby house. **Below:** Purple clematis climbs over the giant grape arbor. (Boston Globe photos/ Pam Berry)

ACKNOWLEDGMENTS

GARDENERS ARE GENEROUS PEOPLE and I've learned from many of them. For their help with this book, I especially want to thank Trish Wesley Umbrell; Tom Strangfeld; John W. Mastalerz, retired professor emeritus in horticulture from The Pennsylvania State University and author of "Notes from John's Garden"; Geoffrey Stocker of Stocker Gardenworks; horticulturist and garden coach Seija Hälvä; Brian McMahon of Natural Tree and Lawn Care of Avon, MA; Bill McKay of Seeds from Italy in Winchester, MA; Daniel Cousins of Nunan the Florist and Greenhouses in Georgetown, MA; John McLoughlin; Deborah Swanson; John Kent; Gary Koller and Tom McCafferty. I'm additionally grateful to Robert Childs, entomology instructor at the University of Massachusetts Amherst; Richard W. Brown, photographer for "Tasha Tudor's Garden" (Houghton Mifflin), and the photo and art departments of the Boston Globe. Most of all: My deep appreciation to my wonderful husband, Robert D. Mussey Jr., for journeying with me through the seasons.

–*Carol Stocker*

Above: A migrating myrtle warbler (Dendroica coronata, also called yellow-rumped warbler) rests amid seaside goldenrod on Nantucket Island. (Boston Globe photo/ Mark Wilson)

THE BOSTON GLOBE ALSO THANKS THE FOLLOWING CONTRIBUTORS:

New England Wild Flower Society. Established in 1900, this esteemed conservation organization runs the largest native plant school in America, plus the remarkable Garden in the Woods botanical garden, Nasami Farm, and sanctuaries across the region. Members receive free admission and discounts, and all purchases support the health of New England's natural habitats. Gardeners seeking nursery-propagated native plants will find them at New England Wild Flower Society's sales nurseries offering 550 species, many of them rare. Contact the New England Wild Flower Society at www.newfs.org or 508-877-7630. Garden in the Woods is at 180 Hemenway Road, Framingham, MA, and Nasami Farm is at 128 North St., Whately, MA.

Massachusetts Audubon Society,
208 South Great Road, Lincoln, MA 01773
(www.massaudubon.org; 781-259-9500).

Park Seed Company,
1 Parkton Ave., Greenwood, SC 29647
(www.parkseed.com; 800-845-3369).

The Netherlands Flower Bulb Information Center
(www.bulb.com).

PW Certified Garden Center
(www.pwcertified.com).

Klehm's Song Sparrow Farm and Nursery,
13101 E. Rye Road, Avalon, WI 53505
(www.songsparrow.com; 800-553-3715).

John Scheepers Flower Bulbs,
23 Tulip Drive, P.O. Box 638, Bantam, CT 06750
(www.johnscheepers.com; 860-567-0838).

Garden Media Group,
P.O. Box 758, Chadds Ford, PA 19317
(www.gardenmediagroup.com; 610-388-9330).

Jackson & Perkins,
1 Rose Lane, Meford, OR 97501
(www.jacksonandperkins.com; 1-877-322-2300).

Keyword Index